ACKNOWLEDGMENTS

It is often said that as we grow older, we look at the world in different ways. In our youth we are convinced that our parents, and in fact all adults, don't know very much. However, the good news is that over time we realize how smart they really are. There is much to learn on a daily basis from everyone we come into contact with. The secret is to listen with an open mind. I'm grateful each day to all who have taught me so much. In writing this book there are many people I'd like to thank for sharing their knowledge and insight. Thanks to:

- ✦ Suki Duggan and Sharon Esche-Irving, for their direct contributions and for sharing their experience from years in the hair-care industry.
- ✦ Beatriz Lopez, my colorist from the Donsuki Salon, who is an artist whose skills I have tested many times in my desire to try "something new."
- ✦ Jane Leiby, who, more than 15 years ago as an Always In Style consultant, developed the first hair-care training manual using the Always In Style concepts of color and body line.
- ✦ Dr. Claire Whitmore and Dr. Janet Hickman, from Lynchburg, Virginia, who offered their expertise during the early years, when I was developing my color concepts.
- ✦ The late Dr. Hugh Mosbacher and his wife, Carole, a special friend who introduced me to the advances in skin-care treatment and the benefits of expert plastic surgery.
- ✦ Dr. Richard Anderson and Dr. Rosa Rasiboni for their understanding, patience, and advice.
  Dr. Friedman-Kein for his work in skin cancer research.
- ✦ Stacey Schieffelin from Models Prefer, for her expertise in makeup and application techniques.
- ✦ Katherine Mecca, a talented makeup artist from the Diane Young Studio, for her support.
- ✦ Dr. Mark Lowenberg and Dr. Larry Rosenthal, two of the leading dentists in New York City, for their contributions and personal care and support.
- ✦ All those at the Lippe Taylor PR agency and the Always In Style staff, who have been supportive of all of my efforts, especially Betty Broder, Elaine Platsman, Monica Brito, Sylvia Ledesma, Becky Jennings, Susan Hughes, Robert Harris, Debra Scott, Jose Flores, and Terry Clarke, and the Desius Group, especially Arun Raj, Sumita Ohri, and Divakar Chandra.
- ✦ My editors and designers at Crisp Publications and Watershed Books.

I'd also like to express a very special thanks to my son, Todd Pooser, whose love, support, and talent have been instrumental in taking Always In Style to its current level of growth and success, allowing me to focus on creating, developing, and promoting my concepts and beliefs.

Last, but not least, I am grateful to my son, Jeff Pooser, and his love, Amy Santos; my sister and my niece, Joan and Molly Molvik; and my wonderful husband, Michael Vaughn, for their love and support of all of my ventures and for being there for me always, each in his or her own special way.

Contents

1 ✦ FINISHING TOUCHES / 9

Factoring Coiffure Into Couture	9
Facing Skin-Care Needs	10
Making Up to Make a Great Impression	10
Enter Suki	11
Finishing Touches	11

2 ✦ WELL DRESSED MEANS WELL TRESSED / 13

Defining the Well-Dressed, Well-Tressed Woman	13
Defining Your Face Shape	16
Balancing Your Face and Hair Shapes	17
Time to Contemplate Your Countenance	17
Minor Face-Shape "Challenges" and Hairstyle Solutions	19

3 ✦ HAIR TEXTURE, TYPE, AND CONDITION / 27

Achieving Healthy, Easy-Care, Easy-Wear Hair   28

    Cleansing   29

    Conditioning and Moisturizing   29

    Using Styling Products   30

How Hair Type Affects Stylability   31

    Coarse and Curly   37

    Coarse, Straight, and Thick   37

    Fine, Straight, and Thin   37

    Fine, Straight, and Thick   38

    Fine and Wavy   38

Virtual Versatility—It's Just Your Style   39

4 ✦ EXPAND YOUR COLOR KNOWLEDGE / 41

Our Ongoing Infatuation with Color   41

Your Color Characteristics   42

    Undertone   42

    Depth   43

    Brightness or Clarity   43

Colors That Complement You   43

Understanding Your Dominant Color Characteristic   44

Choosing a Complementary Hair Color   51

5 ✦ HAIR COLORING—YOUR MOST IMPORTANT FASHION ACCESSORY / 53

It's About Fun, Fashion, Fantasy, and the Future	53
What's New—What's Next	54
The Choice Is Yours	55
Choosing a Complementary Color	55
Deep	57
Light	57
Bright	58
Muted	58
Warm	58
Cool	59
Color Tips, Techniques, and Trends	59
Highlighting	59
Color Shaping	59
Color Blocking	60
Double Identity	60
Hair Painting	60
Smudging	60
Glossing	61
Glazing	61

Caring for Your Color	61
Keep Color Looking Fresh	61
Keep Color-Treated Hair Shiny and Clean	61
Handle Hair Gently	62
Oxidize to Maximize Color	62
Condition, Condition, Condition	62
Salon Versus At-Home Hair Coloring	62
Hair-Color Fashion Show	63

6 ✦ SMART SKIN CARE / 67

Skin—Clearly, the "Canvas"	67
Sorting Out the Truth About Skin Care	68
Healthy Skin, Healthy Lifestyle	69
Sun, Sun, Sun	70
Dry Skin and Wrinkles	70
Professional Skin Care	70
Plastic and Cosmetic Surgery	71
Glycolic Acid Peels	71
Microdermabrasion	72
New Peels	72

Plumping Up and Filling In Lines
and Crevices   73

Botox   73

A Simple, Basic Skin-Care Routine   73

Cleansers   74

Toners   75

Exfoliants   75

Vitamins and Antioxidants   75

Vitamin C   76

Moisturizers   78

Sunscreens   79

Eye Cream   79

Masks and Scrubs   80

Enzyme Peels   80

Self-Tanners   80

Summing Up   81

7 ✦ MODERN MAKEUP AND MORE / 83

Everything Old Is Not New Again   83

Makeup Time—Let the Fun Begin   83

Let Your Coloring Be Your Guide   83

Choosing the Right Products for You   94

Foundation   94

Concealer   95

Powder   96

Blush   97

Eyebrows   97

Eyeliner   98

Eyeshadow   98

Mascara   99

To Curl or Not to Curl   99

Lipstick and Lip Pencil   99

APPENDICES / 107

Eyelash Batting   108

Lip Gunk   109

Faking It   110

Brush Strokes   111

Artful Brows   112

Cutting Edge Bronzer   113

Ray Watch—The ABCs of SPF   114

In the Red   115

The Light Stuff   116

You Go, Curl   117

Artificially Natural   118

Triple Action   119

Personal Profile Questionnaire   121

Color Analysis   122

Bodyline Analysis   124

Hair Analysis   125

Skin Analysis   126

Index   127

Finishing
Touches

I have always believed that the right hairstyle for a particular face shape, good skin care, and correct makeup application are as important to remaining always in style as wearing the right outfit. These concepts are included in my previous books (*Always In Style, Secrets of Style for Women,* and *Successful Style for Men*), but I now consider these critical finishing touches to be so important to making a great first impression that I wrote this book to show you how to get them just right.

FACTORING COIFFURE INTO COUTURE

While I have always admired great hairstyles and healthy shiny hair, for some reason it seemed that there was only so much any woman could do given her hair type. Over the last twenty years I've received many compliments on my hairstyles. Working with my hairstylist, I've been able to achieve the right line and shape for my angular face, and added hair-color highlights that complement my green eyes and golden skin tone. However, my style really didn't change very much from year to year, from day to evening, or from the office to the gym. For a special occasion, I would just try to style my hair to look fuller and spray it a little more.

I have been to many hairstylists, some famous and some not so famous, just to experience their expertise and knowledge. I'm always looking for that new tip to try myself and to evaluate, modify, and

PHOTO: BOYD HARRIS

pass on to my clients. I usually discuss the shape of my cut with my hairstylist, explaining what I want. While generally satisfied, I secretly have always wanted to find that one stylist who would make the big difference so I didn't have to "suggest" a little more angle, or a little more height, or go home and rewash or restyle the cut. In short, someone to make *me* over.

FACING SKIN-CARE NEEDS

My skin has also been a source of consternation. Plagued with blemishes as a teenager, I couldn't wait to grow out of the "problem skin" age. Much to my chagrin, I never did. My skin remained oily, and to complicate matters, it became more sensitive as well. A dermatologist remains on my list of regular appointments to this day. Fortunately, over the years, there has been much progress in skin-care treatments and preventative care. In fact, there are so many effective products available now that instead of being frustrated by having less-than-perfect skin, I get frustrated trying to decide which products to try and what product is best. While it is great to see improved skin products that can give anyone younger-looking skin, the challenge now is to keep my daily skin-care routine simple.

MAKING UP TO MAKE A GREAT IMPRESSION

The greatest reward of a good skin-care regime is the freedom that results from achieving a clear, smooth canvas for the perfect makeup application. The right color makeup, properly applied, should never look like a cover-up or a mask. Today's foundations are easier to apply, look more natural, and are better for your skin than makeup of years past. Learning a few simple application techniques and confidently selecting the right colors and products will help you accent your best features and enhance your unique appearance.

ENTER SUKI

I recently met a very talented hairstylist named Suki Duggan whose Madison Avenue salon, Donsuki, is responsible for some of the most beautiful and trend-setting cuts and hair-color fashion in New York City. Noticing her work in the latest fashion magazines and on television, I decided to ask Suki to provide hair and makeup advice for the Always In Style Portfolio.

I got even more than I'd hoped for. Suki looked at me and said, "You need a few more streaks around your face, a little more fullness, and more angle to your cut—maybe just a little shorter. Let me do it for you."

My session with Suki was magical. Although she stayed within the framework of all of my teachings on line and color, I walked out of her salon looking and feeling ten years younger. My face and eyes looked brighter; my hair was fuller, bouncier, and shinier; and the cut fell effortlessly into place. The compliments followed, giving me the boost we all get when we look "just a little better." My clothes hadn't changed, but I suddenly felt different, more confident.

Could this all be because of a new hairstyle and color? I am convinced that it was. I began to analyze all the aspects of a great hairstyle and continued to meet with Suki. She showed me a few of her special tips and agreed to share her fifteen years of experience by contributing to this book.

FINISHING TOUCHES

There are many excellent new products on the market today that make it easier to have great hair and skin, to look healthy and natural, and to enhance your natural coloring and facial features. The right products and a few simple tips from the experts are all it takes to look and feel great. In this book I'm going to share the results of my own extensive research on hair, makeup, and skin care, along with the expertise of Suki and other professionals, so that you too can experience that magical feeling that comes with knowing you look your very best.

Well Dressed Means
Well Tressed

*D*espite all the changes in modern lifestyles and values, it is still true that within the first thirty seconds of meeting someone, we form an opinion of each other. Of that first impression, 55 percent is based on appearance, 38 percent on body language and voice tone, and 7 percent on what we say. Suki's expertise, plus all the statistics, have convinced me that when we pay attention to how we look (that first 55 percent), we should focus first and foremost on our hair and face, because they are the first things most of us look at when we meet someone new.

Since the right hairstyle and great hair condition is so important to creating that positive first impression, and to your appearance in general, I will now take you step-by-step through a logical approach to achieving your own unique hairstyle, one that will make you look and feel your best.

DEFINING THE WELL-DRESSED, WELL-TRESSED WOMAN

First, let's return to my original definition of "The Well-Dressed Woman"—the one described in my previous books. She wears clothes and makeup that

- ✦ Complement her physically.
- ✦ Express her personality.
- ✦ Are appropriate for the occasion.
- ✦ Are current and fashionable.

To determine your face shape, first look at the typical face shapes on the facing page, and study their characteristics. Now look at yourself in the mirror. Pull your hair back with a headband, and look at your jaw line and cheekbones. Do you see more angles or a softer, more rounded look? If you see a combination of both, which aspect is more appealing to you? Do you like a more angular look or more softness? You can play up your angles or curves if you see some of each. In fact, many famous models have a combination face and can emphasize either their angles or their curves, depending on the clothing or accessories they are modeling. By emphasizing the features and facial characteristics you were born with and feel most comfortable with, you will look and feel your best. Remember, the goal is to enhance your uniqueness. ✦

FACE SHAPES

Think about that woman who walks into a room and makes heads turn. This well-dressed woman makes a statement. She walks with confidence and energy. It is not always easy to define just what makes someone well dressed. I have often heard statements like "She looks coordinated, clean, and well groomed," "Her clothes fit," and "She's wearing the right color." My definition answered the question of how to be well dressed for thousands of women. Now, let's expand that definition by saying that the well-dressed woman also has a hairstyle that does the following:

✦ It complements her physically—it is the right shape and style for her face shape; it corrects any minor problem areas such as a high forehead, a long neck, or a pointy chin; and it makes the best of her unique hair type and condition.

✦ It expresses her personality—it is comfortable, easy to manage, and reflects the total person—her lifestyle, and who she is, inside and out.

✦ It is appropriate for the occasion—it can be styled to reflect day, play, and evening looks.

✦ It is current and fashionable—it reflects a stylish look that is not dated or aging.

Angular face shapes—almond eyes, pointed or slender nose, thin lips, chiseled features

Square

Square jawline

Straight sides

Straight hairline at forehead

Flat forehead
and/or cheek area

Rectangle

Long face

Square jawline

Square forehead at hairline

Flat forehead
and/or cheek area

Diamond

Pointy chin

Prominent cheekbones

Narrow forehead

Triangle

Narrow chin

Prominent cheekbones

Broad or wide forehead

Curved face shapes—round eyes, arched eyebrows, full lips

Round

Soft jawline

Round cheeks

Curved hairline
and forehead

Heart

Wide forehead

Curved hairline or
widow's peak

Narrow chin

Pear

Narrow forehead

Full cheeks

Wide chin

Oval

Soft curves

Curved hairline

Slightly prominent
cheekbones

If your face is more angular (square, rectangle, triangle, or diamond)

◆ Play up the angles and the chiseled features.

◆ Make some simple adjustments for things like a pointy chin or wide forehead.

◆ Create a style that enhances your own personal look.

If your face is more curved (heart, pear, oval, or round)

◆ Create a contoured hairstyle that adds height where needed for balance.

◆ Wear soft bangs to slim a wide forehead.

◆ Maintain the overall softness to complement your face.

PLAY UP THE POSITIVES

Angular faces

DEFINING YOUR FACE SHAPE

Selecting a hairstyle that complements your face shape will guarantee that your hair looks like a natural extension of you, one that enhances your own unique characteristics. We are all familiar with the typical face shapes described in books on style, fashion, and hair: the curved shapes—oval, pear, heart, and round—and the angular shapes—rectangle, square, diamond, and triangle. Remember that whichever shape you were blessed with, all shapes are beautiful. Most of us have a shape that is a combination of curved and angular characteristics.

The oval has always been considered the ideal; stylists and makeup artists are always trying to make face shapes look more oval. Suki and I agree that since face shapes can't be changed, trying to make everyone look alike is silly. Although it is helpful to try to create balance and harmony and to make minor adjustments for small imperfections, we both feel that the best and most comfortable approach is to work with your own unique characteristics. At the Donsuki Salon, Suki "individualizes" each cut according to her client's unique features, lifestyle, and personality.

"It is also important to change our look as we update our total fashion image and change our lifestyle," says Suki. "Many women get stuck in an image groove and resist change, whether it's hair, makeup, or clothes. Most salon experts can preserve your uniqueness while keeping you modern and guiding you fashion forward with subtle changes."

BALANCING YOUR FACE AND HAIR SHAPES

When asked to rate, in order of importance, which features or characteristics were most important to them, 72 percent of the women who responded to a *New Woman* magazine survey said, "Feeling good about my hair." Since I am now convinced that the right hairstyle is so important to creating a positive first impression, and to your appearance in general, I will take you step-by-step through a logical approach to achieving your own unique hairstyle, one that will make you look and feel your best.

Time to Contemplate Your Countenance

Consider the same concepts for hair that apply to your figure. First, you identify your bodyline, and select clothing with the same or similar line or shape—more curved if your body is curved, straighter if you project a straight line. Then make any adjustments needed to compensate for minor figure concerns. For those with narrow shoulders and big hips, for example, add shoulder pads or wear colors or prints on top and dark colors on the bottom. A few simple adjustments can create a taller, thinner, and more balanced silhouette.

Curved faces

More angular hairstyles can be created by

◆ Cutting hair into a point in front of ear.

◆ Cutting hair into a point along the back hairline.

◆ Cutting hair in a bob to create a straight bottom line.

◆ Pulling hair back on one or both sides to accent the angles.

◆ Blunt cutting.

◆ Cutting curly hair in an angular style.

◆ Combining curls and straight areas.

◆ Creating an asymmetrical cut.

More curved hairstyles can be created by

◆ Rounding the shape along back of the hairline.

◆ Creating a circular silhouette.

◆ Cutting wavy or curly hair. in a circular or asymmetrical shape.

◆ Feathered cutting.

◆ Layering.

PLAY UP THE POSITIVES

The same principles apply to your face shape, neck, ears, and overall proportions. If your face is more curved (heart, pear, oval, or round), create a contoured hairstyle that adds height where needed for balance or a soft bang to slim a wide forehead, but keep with the overall softness. Although a round face shape needs a soft hairstyle with some height on top, I do not necessarily suggest replicating the exact face shape in the hairstyle— a round face does not need a round "helmet head." Although your style doesn't need to repeat your exact face shape, a hairstyle with a similar line or shape will complement your features. More angular faces, for example, look great with hairstyles with crisp clean lines and angles.

Now identify your general face shape. Is it more angular or more curved? Next, look at the different angular and curved face shapes in the illustrations on page 15 and identify which one best reflects your unique shape. Remember that your face shape may be a combination of characteristics. Look at the hairstyles that are more curved and more angular in the illustrations on pages 20 through 23. How do they look with the different face shapes? Select the ones that best reflect your overall face shape and that you like best. But before you make a final decision, consider some characteristics that may affect your decision. Some lengths are better for specific face shapes and features, and volume or fullness may be needed to create balance and harmony.

MINOR FACE-SHAPE "CHALLENGES" AND HAIRSTYLE SOLUTIONS

Before we address hair type in Chapter 3, let's consider a few areas that are often overlooked because we tend to look at ourselves in the mirror from one angle only—the front. Suki educates all of her clients about both their best features and those little problem areas that get in the way of maximizing their best look. These minor "challenges" can be easily overcome with some strategic cutting by your stylist and quick styling tips to reproduce at home. Again, don't forget to look at yourself constructively in the mirror from all angles—you may be surprised at what you see. Here are a few tips from Suki to camouflage certain minor problem areas (see illustrations on pages 24 and 25):

✦ For a short neck, keep your hair length medium short to short and try a narrow design line in back.

✦ For a long neck, keep your hair length medium to long and try a design that is wider in back.

✦ For a large nose, bring your hair forward and keep the crown area and back full in order to draw attention away from the nose.

✦ For a flat area on top of the head, layer your cut on top for fullness and height.

✦ For a flat area on the back of the head, add fullness in back with a layered cut or try a volumizer.

✦ For a high forehead, cover or partially cover your forehead with bangs.

✦ For a low forehead, cover your hairline or add height with light bangs.

✦ For a slanting forehead, add full forward-angled bangs.

✦ For protruding ears, wear your hair long enough to cover the front and back of the ears.

A YALE UNIVERSITY STUDY commissioned by Procter & Gamble's Physique hair-care line confirmed that "Bad Hair Days" are real. "Bad hair," according to the study, negatively influences self-esteem, brings out social insecurities, and causes people to concentrate on their negative aspects. Bad hair was defined as hair that sticks out; needs cutting; or is frizzy, damaged, wild, poofy, flyaway, badly cut, bushy, or greasy.

BAD HAIR DAYS

Hairstyles for Angular Face Shapes

Square

*Emphasize your angles with asymmetrical styles
or geometric cuts.*

*Add height to create balance; fullness
on top lengthens your face.*

Add an off-center part or bangs.

Add fullness on the sides to accent your cheekbones

Rectangle

*Emphasize your angles by trying
asymmetrical styles or geometric cuts.*

*Shorten the length of your face with bangs
or an off-center part.*

Add fullness at the sides to accent your cheekbones.

Do not add height or fullness on top.

Diamond

Emphasize your cheekbones with angular hairstyles.

Add width across your forehead with fullness or bangs.

Keep your hair flat at the cheekbones.

Add fullness at chin level.

Triangle

Emphasize your cheekbones with angular hairstyles.

*Use off-center part or bangs to make your forehead
appear more narrow.*

Keep your hair flat at the cheekbones.

Add fullness at chin level.

More Angular Hairstyles

Blunt cut

Asymmetrical cut

Off face style

Bobbed

Angular hairline treatments

Hairstyles for Curved Face Shapes

Round

Emphasize your curves with soft hairstyles.

Add height to balance your neck and face proportions.

Add fullness on top.

Bring your hair forward on the cheeks to reduce width.

Add asymmetrical focus.

Heart

Emphasize your softness and curves.

Use an off-center part to soften and narrow your forehead.

Add fullness at chin level.

Pear

Emphasize your soft curves.

*Add fullness and width at your forehead
to make it appear broader.*

*Bring your hair toward your face at the cheek level
to make your cheeks appear more narrow.*

Keep your hair long enough to soften your chin line.

Oval

*Use softened styles with a slight angle
for interest.*

More Curved Hairstyles

*Straight styles
tapered at ends*

*Soft waves and curls
with blunt cuts*

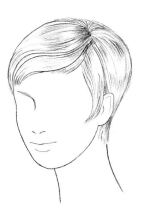

Short feathered cuts

Softened curls

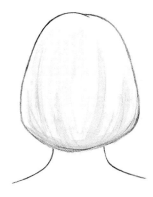

Curved hairline treatments

Hairstyles for Face-Shape Challenges

Flat back of head—
Add fullness in back.

Slanting forehead—
Bring hair forward. Add height and fullness.

Protruding ears—
Cover or partially cover ears.

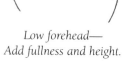

Low forehead—
Add fullness and height.

High forehead—
Try bangs, off-center part, or some hair on forehead.

More Hairstyles for Face-Shape Challenges

Short neck—
Keep hair close or off neck.

Long neck—
Keep hair longer or with softness at neck area.

Large nose—
Add fullness in back and soften front.

Flat top—
Add fullness on top.

To review:

◆ Select a general shape that is best for your curved or angular face shape.

◆ Consider any specific characteristic that may need to be addressed to create a more balanced style.

◆ By adjusting your hair's length, fullness, or shape you will be on your way to selecting a style that is unique and complements your face.

◆ Make adjustments for any particular problem area.

Hair Texture, Type, and Condition

At Donsuki Salon, Suki works with clients who have definite opinions about their own needs and preferences. She loves working with a knowledgeable client who seeks her styling advice, yet has a basic understanding of not only length or style, but hair characteristics such as texture, type, and condition as well.

"At our salons," says Suki, "we focus on educating our clients about their total beauty needs and many options available for hair care, cut, color, texturizing, plus skin care, makeup, and nail care. The more we communicate, the more positive their salon experience will be."

Donsuki Salon handles many celebrities, models, media personalities, and high-powered business executives, people who are knowledgeable about image and most of whom—both men and women—come in with a definite idea of what they want. It's a stylist's job to listen, remain practical, and then guide the client toward a more updated look while staying within her "professional comfort zone." Television news anchors and soap stars, for example, tend to cling to a more stylized look

◆ You have between 100,000 and 150,000 hairs on your head.

◆ Hairs stay on your head from three to seven years.

◆ You can lose as much as 50 percent of your hair before it appears noticeably thinner.

◆ Hair grows about one-half inch per month.

◆ As you get older, hair grows more slowly and thins.

◆ Hair becomes dull when natural oil is stripped from the hair cuticle or as a result of dandruff, which can clog the oil glands.

HEALTHY HAIR FACTS

for years, says Suki. Professional models love to keep their hair long enough to wear many ways for photo shoots and runway shows. Magazine beauty editors tend to be very understated, always soft, blended, and more natural in their overall appearance. Celebrities stick to a public image that sells, while businesspeople prefer to impart a confident look that will make a powerful first impression.

The bottom line is, whether you are famous or not, you want to look modern and "with it"—as fantastic as you possibly can no matter what your age. When clients say to Suki, "Change me—but don't change me," or "Make me look better but don't touch anything," or "Cut my hair long" (a classic request), she simply reads between the lines, she says, and guides them toward the look they want.

ACHIEVING HEALTHY, EASY-CARE, EASY-WEAR HAIR

The key to a great hairstyle is hair that is in excellent condition. To achieve healthy, shiny hair that is easy to care for, you must first understand your hair's basic structure. A hair shaft is composed of three layers: the cuticle, the cortex, and the medulla. The cuticle is the outside layer that protects the cortex. In healthy hair, the cuticle is smooth, allowing light to be reflected, which creates shine. Environmental influences, the chemicals in perms and colors, and heat from blow dryers and curling irons, can damage the cuticle. When this happens, instead of lying flat, the shaft becomes raised and rough, making your hair appear dull and lifeless.

While a healthy diet can promote healthy hair and skin, the only living part of your hair is in the follicle, where new cells are produced to make hair grow. The hair shaft is actually dead, and it can only be treated by conditioning the outer layer and taking steps to prevent further damage.

Cleansing

The first step to healthy hair is to use a gentle shampoo that leaves your hair clean and manageable without stripping all its oils. Selecting the right shampoo can be very confusing given all the products on the market. Each one claims to do something special: there are shampoos for hair that is dry, oily, colored, permed, thin, or thick; shampoos that contain combinations of volumizers, strippers, and conditioners; and on and on.

What most people need, says Suki, is a gentle shampoo that cleans hair of all dirt and excess oil, while retaining the hair's natural moisture. The best shampoos have a protein base and leave hair manageable, with shine and volume. She also recommends avoiding shampoos that contain built-in conditioners, because they tend to be heavy and can weigh hair down.

If you have fine, thin, or oily hair, you will need to wash your hair daily to prevent it from lying flat or try one of the new volumizing shampoos. If your hair has great natural texture and body, you can wash it every other day or so and still maintain volume and movement. You may need to use a clarifying shampoo occasionally to remove buildup from hair sprays. Color-enhancing and volumizing shampoos are a wonderful way to add extra life and color to your hair, but they can be very drying, so you should alternate them with a protein-based shampoo.

Conditioning and Moisturizing

"I can never make this point enough, whether I'm advising a client or giving tips to a magazine beauty editor," explains Suki. "The next step in maintaining healthy hair is to use a conditioner or moisturizer after cleansing for all types of hair. A good moisturizer will condition and strengthen your hair without leaving it overly soft and hard to style."

While there is no conditioner that can repair damaged hair (a good cut is the only solution), a good

STYLING

+ **Seaweed styling gels**—Create shape and soft hold for curly or wavy hair, while adding shine.

+ **Retexturizing mists**—Build volume and protect hair from drying. Some conditioning benefits. Alcohol free.

+ **Jelly beads**—Fragrant styling oils that shine up sleek evening styles, adding glamorous gleam.

+ **Multitasking hairstyling tool sensation**—A new nondrying flat iron made of materials that don't damage, while leaving curly, frizzy hair sleek, smooth, and shiny. This styling tool also helps to "seal in" color.

GREAT NEW PRODUCTS

HAIR CARE

◆ **Seaweed masques**—Intensive deep-conditioning treatments that leave hair looking healthy and feeling luxurious to the touch.

◆ **Instant leave-in conditioners**— Great for hair that is chemically treated. Look for light, nongreasy formulas with SPF for protection from sun damage (especially for lightened hair).

◆ **Color conditioning shampoos**— Refresh color between salon visits (once a week maximum). Tip: Mixing seaweed shampoo in your color conditioning shampoo helps cut color buildup, which leaves hair flat or brassy. The diluted formula refreshes the rich tone and adds shine.

◆ **Cleansing cremes**—Lather luxuriously to gently cleanse and moisturize the hair. Excellent for color-treated hair.

◆ **Botanically correct, all-natural conditioning whips**—Add nourishment and shine using all-natural cream conditioning whips in "flavors" like banana, peach-mango, and fruity framboise. Watch dry hair drink in the goodies and plump up with new vitality.

GREAT NEW PRODUCTS

moisturizer can smooth the hair cuticle and help restore sheen. It will also protect your hair from the elements and prime it for any additional styling products that your hair type may require in order to create a specific style.

Choose a light moisturizer for daily shampooing, and remember that a little bit goes a long way. If your hair clumps together or is limp or flat after styling, you have used too much. For dry or colored hair, work the moisturizer into the hair, comb it through with a wide-tooth comb, and rinse. If you have an oily scalp, use moisturizer on the top layers of your hair only, avoiding the roots and scalp. If your hair is normal or coarse, it does not need daily washing and you need only use moisturizer sparingly, and then only on the ends or top layers.

A deep conditioning treatment, used once a week, says Suki, will provide your hair with the vitamins and minerals necessary to flatten the cuticle and restore shine and elasticity. If you have dry or damaged hair, use a conditioner twice a week. Work it well into your damp hair, then cover your hair and apply heat. If your hair or scalp is oily, apply the conditioner only to the top layers and ends.

Using Styling Products

The greatest advances in hair care over the last ten years have been in treatment and styling products. Permanent and semipermanent colors, perms, straighteners, texturizers, volumizers, and hair sprays all have been improved, allowing you to make your hair look thicker, fuller, shinier, more manageable, and healthier.

Before considering additional styling products, it is important to review the different hair types and recommended cuts and lengths, and to identify the corresponding products that are useful for each.

HOW HAIR TYPE AFFECTS STYLABILITY

In the last chapter you have identified your face shape and some hairstyles that will be complementary. Now it is time to consider your hair type. Is it coarse or fine? Thin or thick? Curly or straight? In between? Let's compare hair texture to fabric texture. Fine hair is like silk, coarse hair is like linen, and the in-between hair texture is like cotton. These comparisons can guide you in thinking about how to treat your particular hair type.

Fine hair is delicate—like silk—and responds to products more quickly than other textures. Each individual hair strand is very thin. Fine hair often hangs flat and lies close to the head, looking thin even if it is thick—that is, there is a lot of it.

Coarser hair is like linen, sturdier and often able to withstand processing much better than fine hair. If your hair can be described as coarse, each individual hair is strong and thick. It will often appear bushy or wiry in humid conditions, and may look dull even after it is just washed.

While your hair type will affect which hairstyle is best for you and easiest to manage, with today's new and improved products you can also create fullness, curl straight hair, straighten curly hair, and add shine. Most important, you can have hair that is healthy, shiny, and easy to care for regardless of your hair type. It all starts at your salon with the right cut just for you.

Coarse and Curly

Layer coarse, curly hair along bottom layer.
Let dry naturally or use a diffuser.
Short styles can be layered on sides and stacked..

Coarse, Straight, and Thick

Blunt cuts and underlayers work well.
Feathered edges allow hair to lie flat.
Use large round brush for softer edges.

Fine, Straight, and Thin

Layers make thin hair look thinner.
Shorter, blunt cuts with stacking add fullness.
Add gel or volumizer at roots.

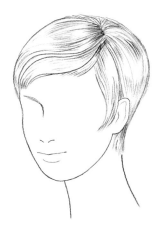

Fine, Straight, and Thick

Blunt cuts show off thick, shiny hair.
Layers add movement.
Tapered and feathered edges add softness.

Fine and Wavy

Stacked and blunt cuts add volume.
Use large round brush to maintain soft wave.
Layers add extra curl to fine, wavy, thick hair.

Coarse and Curly

If your hair is coarse and curly, it will appear thick even if it isn't. Curly hair is often dry, at least on the top layers. To add shine, use a moisturizer to smooth the cuticle and use a deep conditioner once or twice a week.

For the best styling results, apply a gel all over your hair when it is wet. Then let your hair dry naturally or use a diffuser if you want a curly look. For short styles, scrunch your hair with your fingers while drying it with a diffuser, or let it dry naturally for more controlled curls. For straighter styles, use a flat brush, pulling hair through in gentle strokes from scalp to ends. Relaxers can be used to soften and smooth the surface.

It is best to avoid a blunt cut with coarse, curly hair because blunt cuts tend to stick out rather than hang straight. On the other hand, a blunt cut can sometimes work for longer coarse hair because the added weight will hold it down. For medium-length hair, consider a cut that is layered on the bottom, with the top layer being slightly longer. Short cuts can be layered, but be careful that the cut is not too short. Your hair may stick out and may be difficult to control. For coarse hair that is wavy, but not curly, a layered cut will create movement.

Coarse, Straight, and Thick

Coarse, straight hair is often resistant to color and curl, therefore a blunt cut or one with underlayers works especially well for all lengths. Thinning or feathering the hair at the edges often makes thick, straight hair more manageable. For short cuts, avoid too much volume. A layered short cut will show off the thickness and quality and allow the hair to lie flat.

Coarse, straight hair is strong and retains water easily. Therefore, use light moisturizers, and only sparingly. The cuticle is already smooth, so it usually has a healthy sheen. A moisturizer or texturizer will soften the hair and can add movement, as will a soft body wave. When you blow-dry, use a flat or large round brush. A flat brush creates a straighter blunt look. A round brush gives a more rounded edge.

Fine, Straight, and Thin

According to Suki, this type of hair looks better with a blunt cut, wedge, or stacked layers. Long, thin hair has a tendency to look stringy so if you really want some length, don't let it grow any longer than the top of the shoulders. Another style that makes thin hair appear even thinner is a layered cut.

For softer styles, try fringe or some tapered layers around the face and a curved precision cut along the bottom. Although moisturizer is good for conditioning, using too much can make fine, thin hair become flat and limp very easily. For volume try an air, underlayer, or sectional perm; for short hair, use a root perm. Perms add fullness by expanding the hair follicle, as does color.

For styling, apply gel to the roots, adding more at the flat areas of the head, and spray the outer layers with a texturizer. Then bend over and dry your hair loose until it is almost dry. While your hair is still slightly damp, pin it up and begin drying the bottom layers with a round brush. If your hair is already dry, you can use Velcro rollers or electric rollers to add curl or body. If you use electric rollers, wrap the ends of the hair with end papers to protect it. If you use Velcro rollers, never roll them on your hair when it is wet, unless you use end papers.

Fine, Straight, and Thick

Fine hair is delicate, and it curls and colors quickly. Fine hair that is thick layers beautifully and has a lot of movement. Try a chin-length blunt cut, to show off your thick, shiny hair. For a more contoured shape, try some tapering around the face and bangs. Because fine hair can go flat and limp quickly, it benefits from a gentle air perm and is perfect for highlights. Using gel at the roots and texturizer on the outer layers will help maintain volume and fullness.

Fine and Wavy

Fine hair is often wavy but is usually not very curly. Depending on your hair's thickness, follow the advice given above for suggested cuts for fine hair. However, layers often add additional curl and movement to wavy hair. For styling, apply gel all over to achieve a wavier or curlier look. Also pinch in the waves with your fingers, and let your hair dry naturally or use a diffuser. Once your hair is partially dry, you can wind the hair in pin curls to get more curl. For added fullness, apply extra gel to the roots. For a straighter look, apply texturizer and gently blow-dry using a large, round brush.

VIRTUAL VERSATILITY—IT'S JUST YOUR STYLE

A great haircut looks good and is easy to manage, but it should also be versatile. For some reason, however, once we find a style and cut we like we tend to want to wear it the same way all the time. It's comfortable. But it is much more fun to make a few changes depending on the occasion and clothes we are wearing. For example, to create a more sophisticated look, use a gel and slick the hair back, add a new hair comb or accessory, and pull one side back behind the ear or tie it in a low ponytail. There are many options.

Great Transformations

*With your hair in healthy, shiny condition
and a haircut that makes the most of your hair's particular texture and type,
you can create a variety of looks for any occasion.*

PHOTOS: BOYD HARRIS

Expand Your
Color Knowledge

*B*efore going any further on the subjects of hair and hair color, it is helpful to review the original Always In Style color concepts. Since I first expanded the "Four Seasons Color System" introduced by Carole Jackson in her book *Color Me Beautiful*, the validity of my broadened color concepts has been confirmed. Each time I see a makeup success story, like Bobbi Brown's, and find that she agrees with my basic concepts, or see another person look better with just a few simple changes, my mission remains crystal clear: to help people look and feel better about themselves by developing their own style, and to provide the information they need to update their style as they grow both professionally and personally. That mission includes color.

OUR ONGOING INFATUATION WITH COLOR

Over the years, color analysis has had as many critics as advocates. I have to admit that I've often found myself on the side of the critics, much to the chagrin of the image consultant industry. I strongly feel that there are too many unqualified people giving color advice that is wrong or just doesn't make sense. It is wrong to put people into color-coded pigeonholes and expect them to live religiously by a set of thirty swatches dictating their color choices. On the other hand, I know that color plays a very important role in personal appearance. There is an ongoing infatuation with color. Women are drawn to cosmetics counters and drawn to the new colors that are introduced each fashion season.

Certain colors, tones, and shades do look better on one person than another. For example, red is perhaps the most striking color that Suki can wear, especially against her dark, shiny, long hair and huge dark eyes. I, on the other hand, look dreadful in bright red and even worse in shades of pink (which Suki also wears well). On my lips, pink, quite frankly, looks cheap. Bright reds aren't any better—they make me look like a clown! But because I understand why these colors don't work, I can select a particular version of pink or red, such as a warm pink or a shade of brick red, to achieve a look that is unique and flattering on me—warmer, more muted, or more blended.

By understanding the characteristics of color and your own coloring, you can successfully wear all colors in a unique and individual way. I will avoid wearing a pink suit, for example, because it doesn't suit my personality, and I prefer neutral colors. I really am not a fan of pink lipstick, but in the last several years, when soft subtle lips in pink tones were in fashion, I switched to a pinkish beige lipstick that looked like a soft warm pink on me and updated my look.

Color for hair is another important fashion element. While statistics vary, some market surveys indicate that as many as 90 percent of the women in the United States have used some type of hair color product, and more than thirty-five million American women have color-treated hair. Before I get into different hair color options, however, let's review some color characteristics to determine how you can make the best color choices and how you can wear virtually any color.

YOUR COLOR CHARACTERISTICS

All colors are made up of the three primary colors: red, blue, and yellow. All colors also have three characteristics: undertone, depth, and brightness or clarity.

Undertone

In describing color undertone, we often hear the terms *warm* and *cool*. Warm colors have a golden or yellow base, and cool colors have a blue base. However, there are many colors that appear to have equal amounts of cool and warm. If we mix equal parts of blue (a cool color) with yellow (a warm color), we could say that we have an equal mix of warm and cool. Consider the color red. As yellow is added to red you get warm reds, and as blue is added you get cool reds. But true red appears neither warm nor cool, but "in between."

Technically, the amounts of yellow or blue in a color can be measured precisely. However, you and I do not live in a laboratory. There are many colors that appear to be in between. In addition, we all see color differently. Some people can retain a color image longer than others, but in general the average person retains a color image for about thirty seconds. Also, colors change their appearance when combined with other colors. Put true red next to golden yellow and it looks warmer; put it next to bright blue, and it appears cooler. By understanding undertone, you will be able to select colors that complement your undertone.

Depth

All colors can be defined in terms of how light or dark they appear. A blue-red goes from the lightest powder pink to a deep burgundy, all cool colors. An orange-red ranges from the lightest peach to the darkest rust, all warm colors. And if we take a true red and lighten or darken it, we will get a light coral pink or a deep mahogany. These colors appear neither all warm nor all cool. Understanding how to use deep and light colors will give you more opportunities to use colors in a complementary way.

Brightness or Clarity

All colors have either a bright, clear look; a drab, dusty, or muted look; or something in between. Compare a bright magenta or fuchsia to mauve. Most muted colors are soft and subtle; they are often referred to as "no-color" colors, or complex colors. Some of us look better in bright colors; others in more muted.

COLORS THAT COMPLEMENT YOU

Just as colors have three characteristics, so does our own coloring—skin tone, hair color, and eye color. Just as colors cannot always be divided into warm and cool, neither can most of us, because most people tend to have some characteristics of each. You may have golden blonde hair, cool blue eyes, and a very neutral-appearing skin tone; or dark hair, dark eyes, and olive skin, which appears more golden when you wear warm tones and cool when you wear cool tones.

It is best to look at your most dominant characteristic and realize that colors that have the same or a similar characteristic will be complementary. Use these colors as the foundation from which to build your preferred palette. Other colors can be used to soften or brighten your look, make you look more dramatic or more conservative, or create a particular mood or evoke an emotion.

UNDERSTANDING YOUR
DOMINANT COLOR CHARACTERISTIC

Understanding your dominant color characteristic will give you the ability to select colors, especially makeup and hair colors, that will always create balance and harmony and look complementary on you. The basic color types are described below (for more information on your coloring, refer to my previous books *Always In Style* and *Secrets of Style*).

+ **Deep**—The deep characteristic is the easiest to see. A deep person has dark hair and eyes. Skin tone ranges from very light to deep olive. There is a strength to her coloring. Dark colors create balance and harmony.

+ **Light**—The light person has light to medium blonde hair, ash to golden in hue; light to medium skin tone; and blue, green, or blue-green eyes. Light to medium colors are complementary and create harmony and balance.

+ **Bright**—The bright person has a bright, clear look resulting from the contrast between her dark hair, very light skin tone, and clear blue or green eyes. There is a delicate quality about this woman's coloring that is complemented by clear colors and lots of contrast.

+ **Muted**—Muted coloring has a soft, but not delicate, quality that is projected with either light ash blonde hair and dark brown eyes or medium brown eyes and hair. Skin tone ranges from a very pale, no-color look to soft pink or golden. The complex or no-color colors are very complementary on this woman, creating little contrast and a more subtle neutral tone.

+ **Warm**—The truly golden person has red or golden hair; warm green, hazel, or aqua eyes; and obviously golden, peach, or bronze skin tone. Freckles are often an added feature. Golden, yellow-based colors blend with the richness of her coloring.

Colors

THE DEEP PALETTE contains strong, rich colors that range from midtones to those that appear almost black. They can be clear and bright or more muted and can be warm or cool. The true shades are also complementary. Use very light, icy colors for contrast or as accents.

Characteristics

Caucasian
Hair—Black to deep brown, chestnut, auburn; may have warm undertones

Eyes—Brown, brown-black, hazel, rich green or olive; not blue

Skin—Beige, olive, bronze

African-American
Hair—Black, brown-black

Eyes—Black, brown-black, red-brown, brown

Skin—Blue-black, deep brown, rose-brown, mahogany, bronze

Asian
Hair—Blue-black, black, brown-black, chestnut, dark brown

Eyes—Black, brown-black, red-brown

Skin—Olive, bronze, beige

DEEP

The light palette ranges from soft pastels to midtones. The colors can be clear and bright or soft and muted. In the light and middle range, colors do not appear too bright. Complementary shades range from slightly warm to a rosier tone. Darker shades should be used away from the face or in combination with lighter tones.

Characteristics

Caucasian

Hair—Light to dark, ash, or golden blonde

*Eyes—Blue, blue-green, green aqua;
not deep hazel or brown*

Skin—Ivory to soft beige, pink, or peach; little contrast

African-American

*Hair—Soft black, brown-black, light brown,
red-brown, ash brown*

Eyes—Soft black, brown, rose-brown

Skin—Light brown, caramel, rose-beige, cocoa

Asian

*Hair—Brown-black, ash brown,
brown, soft black*

*Eyes—Red-brown, brown-black,
black, gray-black*

Skin—Rose-beige, ivory, pink, peach, beige

Colors

LIGHT

THE BRIGHT PALETTE is one of clear, true primary colors. They range from midtones to deeper tones that remain clear and do not appear muted or grayed down. Use deep colors with white or a bright color near the face. Two deep colors together or muted shades will appear heavy.

Characteristics

Caucasian

Hair—Medium to dark; brown, from ash to golden; chestnut; black

Eyes—Bright and clear: blue, blue-green, turquoise, gray, light hazel

Skin—Light: ivory, porcelain, or beige; translucent quality

African-American

Hair—Black, brown-black, ash brown

Eyes—Black, brown-black

Skin—Light-medium brown, deep beige, cocoa, caramel

Asian

Hair—Black, brown-black, dark brown

Eyes—Black, brown-black, hazel

Skin—Ivory, porcelain

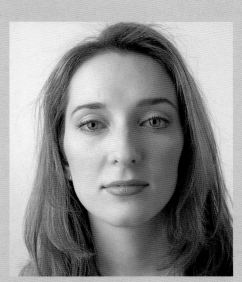

Colors

BRIGHT

THE MUTED PALETTE contains soft, blended, grayed-down colors that range from midtones to rich, deep colors. Often lighter shades work well. Muted colors can lean toward the warm or cooler tones.

Characteristics

Caucasian

Hair—Medium range:
medium ash brown to dark ash blonde

Eyes—Grayed green, hazel, brown-green, brown
(medium to dark), green, or teal

Skin—Ivory, beige, bronze;
golden freckles and ruddiness common

African-American

Hair—Brown, ash brown, brown-black

Eyes—Brown-black, black, gray-brown,
hazel, rose-brown

Skin—Light brown, cocoa, rose-brown, beige; opaque,
freckles, absence of strong color

Asian

Hair—Brown, mahogany, ash brown, soft black

Eyes—Brown, rose-brown, hazel,
brown-black, gray-brown

Skin—Beige, rose-beige, bronze; absence of color;
opaque, freckles

Colors

MUTED

Colors

THE WARM PALETTE contains colors with obvious golden undertones that range from light to deeper rich tones. They can be bright and clear but darker shades often appear more muted. Some true colors can be added to the palette for variety, especially greens and blues.

Characteristics

Caucasian

Hair—Medium range:
blonde or brown with gold, red, or strawberry highlights

Eyes—Warm:
green, hazel, brown, topaz, blue-green, teal

Skin—Golden: beige, ivory, bronze; may have freckles

African-American

Hair—Brown, golden brown,
brown-black, chestnut

Eyes—Warm brown, topaz,
deep brown, hazel

Skin—Bronze, caramel, mahogany, golden brown,
light brown, brown; freckles

Asian

Hair—Golden brown, auburn,
dark brown, chestnut

Eyes—Warm brown, brown-black,
hazel, deep brown, topaz

Skin—Golden beige, ivory, bronze; freckles

WARM

THE COOL PALETTE contains colors that have blue undertones and range from midtones to deep shades. The true colors are often complementary additions to this palette. Colors with obvious warm undertones should be used in combination with cool colors and away from the face.

Characteristics

Caucasian

Hair—Ash brown (dark to medium), silver, or salt-and-pepper

Eyes—Rose-brown, gray-brown, gray-blue

Skin—Beige, rose-beige, pink

African-American

Hair—Black, ash brown, blue-black

Eyes—Brown-black, black, gray-brown, rose-brown

Skin—Rose-brown, gray-brown, cocoa, dark brown, soft blue-black

Asian

Hair—Black, blue-black, brown-black, ash brown, dark brown, salt-and-pepper

Eyes—Black, gray-brown, rose-brown

Skin—Pink, rose-beige, gray-beige; sometimes sallow

Colors

COOL

◆ **Cool**—There are very few, if any, all-cool people. The younger we are, the more golden tones we have in our hair and eyes. It is only when we start to age that we lose pigment in our hair, begin to gray and lose color in our eyes and skin tone. It is often best to add some warm tones to create a younger look. However, there are women with ash or gray hair, rose skin tone, and cool blue or gray eyes who appear to be more cool than warm. Cooler colors are complementary.

CHOOSING A COMPLEMENTARY HAIR COLOR

Most women use color to cover their gray hairs, others want to add highlights, and some just want a dramatic change in their look. Although more than 90 percent of American woman have used some type of hair color, unfortunately many of these experiences ended in disaster. Poor results usually are due to incorrect application, which can damage the hair, or poor color choice.

With advances in the quality and performance of hair-coloring products, it is now easier than ever to make an immediate positive change in your image. When applied correctly, a new color can give texture and body to thin or limp hair; add sheen, depth, and movement; enhance existing hair color; brighten your face; make you look younger; and create a more fashion-forward look. Used incorrectly, hair coloring can damage the hair, making it look dry and strawlike, with little or no sheen or movement. A poor coloring job can also give you a head of hair that looks unrelated to your natural coloring, which can make you look older, like a fashion victim, outdated, or just plain cheap.

Whatever your reason for deciding to enhance or change your hair color, it should look natural. If you look at a young child's hair in the sunlight, you will see a healthy shine, often with many different shades of warm and golden highlights. The younger we are, the more warmth we have in our hair and skin tone. As we age, our hair, eyes, and skin lose pigment and some of the glow. Restoring some of this richness creates the most natural, healthy look. Lightening the hair one or two shades or adding subtle highlights will add luster, brightness, and movement. In the next chapter, I will review current hair-coloring techniques and show you how to select a color that works for you.

Hair Coloring—Your Most Important Fashion Accessory

*I*t has taken many years for hair color to become a truly acknowledged part of total fashion. At the Donsuki Salon, it is a rare occasion when a client who has come in for a cut leaves without a beautiful touch of color to show off the cut and bring out her eye color and skin tone. This increased consumer acceptance of "coloring your hair" both at the salon and at home got a tremendous fashion boost in the media in the early 1970s, when highlighting came into vogue with a new, more natural look that women loved. More than thirty-five million American women now use some form of color, and the hair-color business is booming. Hair color of all kinds is considered an important fashion accessory—"makeup" for the hair. The right color can transform a good cut into a fabulous look.

IT'S ABOUT FUN, FASHION, FANTASY, AND THE FUTURE

Suki has observed that the reasons women color their hair have changed dramatically in just the past several years. Many women love color because it changes the texture of their hair, making it appear thicker and more luxurious to the touch. Others use clear color glazes and glosses to add shine to dull hair. Teens love the fun of color choices, from totally bold-colored slashes and sections to subtly painted-on pastels that blend the bangs and frame the face. The Baby Boomer generation is using color more and more to maintain a modern image and to keep looking as young as they feel as they reel into middle age. Other women use color to dramatically change their image. Seniors often use it to enhance their own gray or to go softly lighter with natural blending highlights. Let's face it: hair color isn't just used to cover gray anymore. It's about fun, fashion, fantasy, and the future.

WHAT'S NEW—WHAT'S NEXT

Today, hair coloring presents a world of choices and fresh fashion options. From classic to contemporary, American haircuts and colors take their cues from the runways of Paris, London, and Milan and from the style of public personalities in popular music, film, and sports around the world.

Currently, hair-color fashions reflect natural looks, a combination of beautiful multitones and lights blended throughout one head of hair. Color is used to create interesting contrasts and contours that shape a cut, light up the eyes, enhance a face shape, or bring out a person's true color personality. Strategically placed highlights accent surface layers, while inner sections of the hair glow from within, with rich, deeper color shadows for added dimension.

Solid or one-color looks are definitely part of fashion today (especially among younger women), although solid hair color is often perceived as too heavy or harsh, often aging, and not very interesting, considering the alternatives. Yesterday's redhead today has a softer blend of amber-red or a deeper ginger-copper. Blonde is more muted or matte, containing multiple tones of butterscotch, honey, or vanilla blonde. Brownettes are spiced up with berry, raisin, or cognac hues or surfed up with sandy gold sunlights. Contemporary brunettes often opt for subtle shades of aubergine or mahogany with magnificent shine.

Extreme hair color, inspired by the style-conscious men and women of Australia and the United Kingdom, has also had tremendous impact on the American market. The bright greens, pinks, oranges, golds, and electric blues express the individuality of teen through twenty-something consumers and their Baby Boomer parents have also noticed this trend. This mass self-expression and color explosion is even turning the heads of the color-shy and inspiring them to be more daring. They may not be going vivid green or blue, but they are making less conservative, more exciting color choices.

THE CHOICE IS YOURS

Like clothing fashions, there are new color trends in hair, makeup, and nails for every season. Fashion and image experts suggest you get some type of hair-color update for spring-summer and fall-winter, along with a great new haircut or style to keep you looking fresh. The changes don't have to be drastic—just enough to complement your new clothes, your new makeup, and your new nail color. Any type of hair can be highlighted. Thin hair will look thicker and fuller; thick hair will have more movement and depth.

With the use of permanent hair color you can apply small streaks of color throughout. The streaks look more natural when done in several different shades. Two or three different shades of blonde can be used on lighter hair, and red, honey, or bronze streaks on brunettes.

Brunettes should avoid light blonde streaks and unnatural burgundy shades, however. Lighter streaks frame the face, but they should be placed where the sun would naturally lighten the hair color. Overall "frosting," which was so popular in the 1970s and 1980s, looks outdated and unnatural.

One word of caution for older women: avoid colors that are too dark, especially around the face. As we age we lose pigment in our skin, eyes, and hair, which gives us a softer, lighter look. Trying to match the color that your hair was when you were twenty or thirty years old does not work when you reach fifty or sixty or older. The contrast is too strong and looks harsh.

CHOOSING A COMPLEMENTARY COLOR

With the many different hair colors available today, it is possible to alter your hair to any color you want. Many celebrities change their hair color monthly or even weekly. Depending on fashion trends, your own personality, and your personal color preferences, you have many options. Some will be more complementary than others. The color recommendations in the illustrations on page 56 include only those options that create more-natural looks and those that will safely complement your particular color characteristics. The rest is up to you.

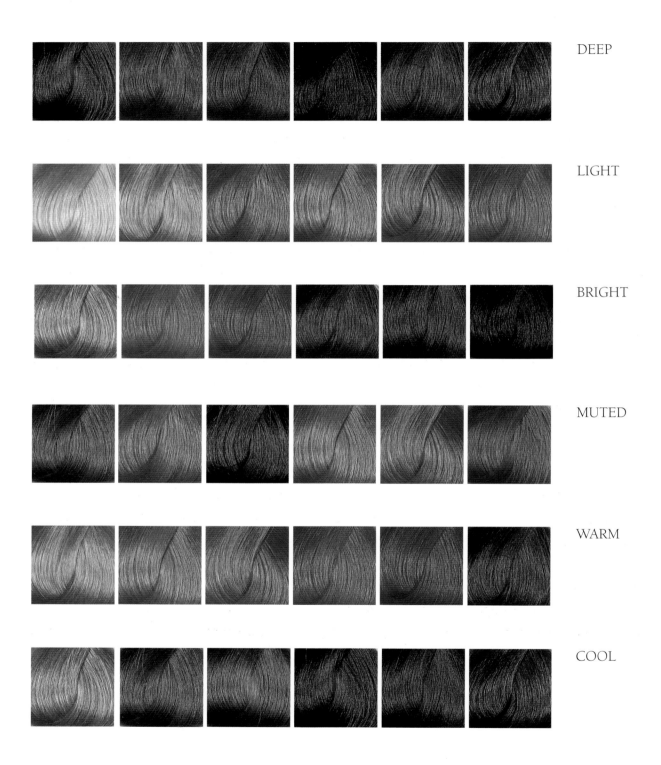

DEEP

LIGHT

BRIGHT

MUTED

WARM

COOL

Deep

Dark hair and eyes;
light, medium, olive, or deep skin tone

If your coloring is deep and you want to change or enhance your natural hair color, try auburn, mahogany, chestnut, or copper tones. Select a shade similar in depth to your natural color. Remember, if you use a temporary color in a red tone you will not become a redhead. Your hair will not appear red, but will have a natural sheen. Your natural color will not lighten, but it will pick up a subtle hint of the color. If you prefer to lighten just a little, try some highlights using colors one or two shades lighter than your natural shade, keeping your overall range in the deep category.

If you want to lighten your hair a lot, you will need to use a permanent color. For those with dark hair and eyes and medium to deep skin tone, the medium to deep tones are most complementary. Light blonde tones are not usually recommended for those with deep coloring. If your skin tone is very light or porcelain, a medium blonde shade can be complementary but will be difficult to keep up (see the light shades).

If you want to cover your gray, try a chestnut or dark brown shade that is slightly lighter than your original shade. Remember to mix at least two different colors for a more natural look. As you age and your overall coloring softens, avoid black and black-brown shades, because they tend to look harsh.

Light

Medium to light blonde hair;
blue, gray, green, or blue-green eyes; light to medium skin tone

If your coloring is light, you can add medium to light warm-blonde shades for depth and richness. Highlights in several shades of blonde will create movement and sheen. Light and ash blondes can go darker or warmer. Be careful with ash tones, however, because they can look flat and make you look older. Try honey or strawberry shades for a warmer look.

If your eyes are a bright shade of blue or green you will find that a Titian red, copper, or deep golden blonde will also be complementary, changing your light coloring to bright (see the bright shades).

Bright

Medium to dark brown or black hair;
bright blue, green, hazel, or turquoise eyes; and light skin

If you are bright, your skin tone is very light porcelain or ivory, and there is contrast between your hair and skin. Most brights have a neutral skin tone, thus they can go warmer or cooler in their hair-color choices. Complementary shades are the Titian reds, auburns, and coppers. Alternatively, dark browns and chestnuts add contrast and sheen. Highlights that are one or two shades lighter than your natural coloring also work well.

Because of your light skin and bright, clear eyes, you can lighten to an ash or golden blonde. You will find that the light hair color softens your look slightly and expands your color choices to include light colors, brights, and some warms depending on the shade of blonde you use (see the light and warm shades).

Muted

Light to medium blonde or brown;
hazel, gray, or brown eyes; neutral skin tone

If your coloring is muted, you have a softness to your overall appearance and your coloring is complemented by dusty and soft colors. Your coloring is not as delicate as the light person who has lighter eyes. Therefore, you can choose medium to deep shades in both warm and cool tones. High- and lowlights will work very well, creating a gentle but sophisticated look.

Try adding several shades of blonde with lighter shades around your face. Chestnut and honey shades will also complement your coloring and will allow you to use deeper and warmer shades of makeup and clothing. Avoid bright Titian shades.

Warm

Golden skin and hair;
hazel, golden brown, or green eyes

If your coloring is golden, you can add copper, golden, and honey shades to enrich and enhance your hair coloring. If your eyes are a bright color, go brighter or lighter, choosing Titian reds, auburn, or golden blondes. If your eyes are a soft brown or hazel, try auburn, copper, or honey shades. Golden blonde highlights will also work well. Adding neutral blonde streaks will soften deeper or red shades and create a more muted look (see muted shades).

Cool

Ash brown or blonde hair; gray, brown, or gray-blue eyes; and pink or beige skin tone

As you have already learned in the discussion of color characteristics in Chapter 3, cool coloring is often misunderstood. We all have some warm tones in our hair and skin. They are often subtle or indiscernible, and they tend to fade as we get older, giving us a softer, cooler tone. Therefore it is a good idea to restore some of this warm coloring when selecting hair color and makeup. At the very least, choose a neutral shade, adding some variation of color to the ash base.

Ash tones are created by adding purple or blue to the color mixture. Don't let the color go too flat or too blue, however. If your hair is gray or graying, consider adding a golden or natural blonde or brown to cover the gray. Avoid blacks and deep shades, because they are too strong for the softer look that the "cooler" color creates.

COLOR TIPS, TECHNIQUES, AND TRENDS

You will love the choices you have today of the most current hair-color fashion looks. They are in all the magazines, on the runways, and in films—all available to you for the asking. Let's take a look at some of the most current hair-color fashion looks. The techniques that follow are among the most popular methods offered at Donsuki and many other salons throughout the country.

Highlighting

Highlighting, lightening selected strands, is the most popular hair-color method because it looks so natural. It's a way to play up and duplicate what Mother Nature already gave us: beautiful light and dark tones throughout our hair. This technique can warm hair with fine, coppery highlights or add shining glints of blonde like those naturally lightened by the sun. An alternative technique is lowlighting: instead of lightening strands, a slightly darker color is added to give the hair depth, achieving a tone-on-tone effect.

Color Shaping

In color shaping, the colorist uses hair color to add dimension to a haircut by creating contrasting shadows and light. Strategic color placement creates shapely illusions in regard to the cut

As a hairstylist, Suki has changed her hair-color terminology to make the language of coloring more consumer friendly and to reflect its acceptance as part of fashion. Hair color has never been perceived as more fun, more important, or simply "good for the hair." Now it's time for you to brush up on the new language of color.

◆ We don't "dye" our hair, we "color treat" it.

◆ Color is a "cosmetic" that conditions our hair, not just a "chemical" we put on it.

◆ We no longer have "roots," we have "regrowth" areas.

◆ Terms like "highlights," "high-lift tints," and "two-step color" have replaced words like "double-process blonding" and "streaking."

◆ We "lighten," our hair, we don't "bleach" it.

◆ A color "makeover" is now color "modernizing."

◆ "Covering up gray" is now often referred to as "executive blending."

BRUSHING UP ON THE NEW LANGUAGE OF COLOR

itself, making it look even straighter, rounder, wavier, or heavier.

Color Blocking

The color blocking technique makes use of sectional coloring, either lightening or adding color to whole sections or "blocks" of hair, such as the back or sides. This technique takes its cue from current clothing design. It also makes use of permanent color.

Double Identity

Double identity is a technique that creates "two-way" hair color, which varies with the way you wear your hair. The colorist uses strategic placement of multiple highlights that will make your hair look different depending on how you wear it: brushed forward, swept to one side, or pulled up.

Hair Painting

With the hair-painting technique, the colorist accents the style by brushing color and light (highlights) onto the hair's surface using a special brush. If you have bangs, for example, your colorist can paint soft edges of light along the bottom of your bangs, or outline your curls and waves. This hair-painting technique is called "tipping."

Smudging

Smudging adds soft, diffused, muted color to give intriguing, smoky overtones that "smolder" from within.

Glossing

Glossing is a quick five-minute "refresher" of permanent color and conditioner. It brightens the color and maximizes the shine.

Glazing

Glazing adds a fast, clear coat of noncolor that adds surface shine or brilliance to the hair, giving it a healthy-looking, highly reflective sheen.

CARING FOR YOUR COLOR

Maintaining great hair color is easier these days, thanks to new hair-care products formulated for color-treated hair. Gone are the days when color fades quickly and becomes drab. The new color-refresher shampoos and conditioners, used between color applications, keep hair looking healthy, shiny, and color-rich for weeks and even months, depending on your hair's length and the coloring technique used. Here are some more tips for maintaining your new color.

Keep Color Looking Fresh

Semipermanent color should be refreshed every four to six shampoos. Permanent all-over color should be touched up about every four weeks. Highlights need refreshing only four to six times a year. Check out the in-between color refreshers, such as shampoos, conditioners, and styling mousses that are specially formulated for each color category.

Keep Color-Treated Hair Shiny and Clean

Dirt, oil, hair-setting aids, and hair sprays coat the hair shaft and make the color look slightly duller or flat. Thus it is important to shampoo regularly.

WHEN CHANGING your hair color, remember to balance your eyebrow color with your hair.

For dark hair, keep your eyebrows one or two shades lighter than your hair.

If you are going blonde, keep your eyebrows one or two shades darker than your hair color.

TIP

Handle Hair Gently

When you color your hair, you alter its texture. Your hair actually has a fuller quality because coloring "opens up" the cuticle of each hair shaft. This open texture makes hair more likely to grab other strands and get tangled when washed. To avoid breakage or split ends, avoid rough handling, and don't force out the tangles and snarls while your hair is still damp. Consider using a detangler instead.

Oxidize to Maximize Color

Hair needs to interact with air (oxygen) to blend and achieve ultimate color richness. Give your hair at least twenty-four to forty-eight hours to oxidize after the color has been applied in order to see your final hair-color result. Don't shampoo for a couple of days, if possible.

Condition, Condition, Condition

Color-treated hair needs to be conditioned or remoisturized after every shampoo to maintain natural oils and healthy glow (much like moisturizing dry skin after cleansing). You don't need to condition your entire head each time. Simply focus on the area of the hair that needs the most replenishing—the ends. Work conditioner through only the surface and ends. Deep-condition once or twice a month.

SALON VERSUS AT-HOME HAIR COLORING

It is true—coloring your hair at home has become much easier and more convenient thanks to new product technology. No matter how great the product, however, nothing compares to the skill of a salon colorist. A professional colorist can give you the best results, especially for the techniques that require more expertise, precision, and maintenance. One look at the gorgeous work of the Donsuki salon colorists in the photographs on pages 63 through 65 reaffirms this belief.

If you're considering updating your hair color, I strongly recommend that you consult with your hairstylist and colorist. Often, a consultation is complimentary, and your salon expert will give you an objective and up-to-date evaluation of "what's hot" and "what's not" in cut and color fashion.

An experienced professional will factor in your lifestyle, individual features, fashion personality, and concerns about cost, maintenance, and overall commitment. It is then possible to maintain your color at home.

HAIR-COLOR FASHION SHOW

With so many options available today, it's always possible to find a way to turn your great cut into an even greater look with hair color. Let's take a look at some gorgeous hair-color fashion effects now available.

Blonde

Before **After**

*Beatriz Lopez of Donsuki Salon foiled in medium-blonde and honey lowlights,
adding shine and movement.
Lisa Galanti's cut added a graduated shape with long vertical layers and thicker bangs.*

Shades of blonde

Red

Before

After

Franco Carollo enhanced this blonde's hair with strawberry blonde streaks.
Joseph Perricone created a sleek bob and styled the hair for lift and height.

Shades of red

Brunette

Before   **After**

Beatriz Lopez foiled in heavy copper highlights.
Suki Duggan snipped off two inches and added lots of under-layers for curl control.

Shades of brown

Smart
Skin Care

*N*ow that your hair looks great, it's time to talk about skin. Skin is a human's largest sensory organ, and it reveals much about us, particularly our overall general health. Beautiful, smooth, glowing skin is one of the first things that people notice when they look at a woman or man. My dream has always been to have a beautiful complexion. This is because of my own experience suffering through years of teenage acne. Determined to find a miracle solution, I spent thousands of dollars on doctors, medicines, and treatments.

SKIN—CLEARLY, THE "CANVAS"

Like me, most people have a particular facial or body feature, area, or characteristic that they are more sensitive about than any other. Women tend to zero in on hips, legs, nose, or complexion. Many people don't know how many excellent skin-care services and products are available from dermatologists and at local salons and day spas to help achieve that healthy, glowing complexion. In the last thirty years, there has been tremendous progress in medications and techniques that can prevent breakouts, better maintain the skin, prevent permanent damage, and repair scarring.

Although I lived through the trauma of bad skin, I was lucky to work with excellent dermatologists and plastic surgeons, who helped me improve my skin and guided me in my continued research

Vitamin E provides front-line antioxidant defense and gives your skin a silky softness.

Vitamin C supports the body's natural defenses against the UV-induced breakdown of collagen.

Vitamin A increases your skin's natural moisture retention.

Panthenol (pro-vitamin B5) boosts your skin's suppleness and elasticity.

Grape seed extract interrupts the enzyme reactions that can break down skin-firming collagen.

Superoxide dismutase (SOD) neutralizes the free radicals that visibly age your skin the fastest.

Beta glucan soothes environmental irritation.

SOURCE: SKAKLEE RESEARCH LABS.

SKIN-CARE PROTECTION

and evaluation of new skin-care treatments and products. A consultation with your salon esthetician about basic skin care can make a huge difference in your skin's condition and appearance, no matter what your age. Of course, it may be necessary to consult a dermatologist for more complicated or specialized skin-care needs, and your esthetician may be able to refer you to just the right expert.

SORTING OUT THE TRUTH ABOUT SKIN CARE

In this new computer and information age, there is abundant, in-depth information available on almost any subject. There is only one problem with this wealth of knowledge: too much information and too little time. We are already so busy with work, families, and, hopefully, exercise and fitness programs, that there is little extra time for fun and relaxation, much less keeping up on all the subjects that interest us. Thus we need to rely on services and experts in various fields to do the research, sift through the volumes of information, and provide accurate information and nonbiased facts. Armed with reliable information, we can make the right decisions for our own situations and needs.

The need for reliable information is especially true in a field such as skin care. Many skin-care treatments do not fall under the category of medicine and are therefore not regulated by the U.S. Food and Drug Administration. Skin-care companies are in the business of making money. They pay huge sums of money to public relations and advertising firms to pitch story lines in the media to convince us that their products will work miracles. Much of the hype is just not true. However, there are some remarkable products available today, and there is much we can do to look healthier and younger and prevent further damage to our skin.

In addition to expert advice, as soon as the newest and latest products hit the market, I've got my credit card ready. I like to personally hear the sales pitches and try the products, and despite the disappointments when a product doesn't live up to the hype, I still believe in keeping up with the market. Over time, my team of experts has expanded and I rely on them more and more. I know that my basic skin-care products work well and are right for me, but I want to confirm and update my product information on a regular basis.

I am pleased to pass on the valuable information I have accumulated over the years, to summarize my findings, and to recommend some simple skin-care guidelines. I hope that this chapter will answer questions, provide a basis for sorting through the products and hype, and prepare your skin for the fun part of trying makeup to enhance your natural beauty. I know you, too, will continue to try new products that promise miracles, but perhaps I will save you from a few mistakes.

HEALTHY SKIN, HEALTHY LIFESTYLE

It has been said that your health can be seen in your skin. Glowing skin requires a healthy diet, lots of water, exercise, and plenty of rest. Smoking and alcohol wreak havoc on skin, causing wrinkles, lines, and discoloration. There is no getting around the fact that we must take care of our bodies and be more diligent as each year goes by. All the cleansers, creams, peels, and facelifts in the world will do no good if you do not live a healthy lifestyle. So perhaps now is the time to make the commitment to start taking care of yourself, inside and out. Start today with a healthy diet and exercise program, and take time to relax.

In young healthy skin, new cells are generated in the deep structures of the skin, migrate to the top, and are sloughed off every thirty to forty-five days. Plumper, healthier cells then surface, making the skin look smoother. As you get older this process slows. If you have dry skin, the dead cells build up on the surface, making wrinkles and lines more pronounced. Moisturizers and creams only make these dead cells stick together, making it even more difficult for them to be sloughed off. With oily skin these dead cells get stuck together and clog pores, creating bumps and blotches. In both cases, flat misshapen cells make the surface appear rough and lined. These dead cells must be removed so they can be replaced by round, moisture-filled, smoother cells, creating a softer, smoother skin surface.

Sun, Sun, Sun

Nothing feels better than waking up to a bright, beautiful, sunny day and feeling that wonderful warm sun on your face. It makes you feel uplifted, healthy, happy, and alive. However, over and over again you hear the warning—"Stop! Stay out of the sun." The facts are indisputable. The sun is the primary cause of aging skin and skin cancer. How could something that feels so good be so bad? It doesn't seem fair. And yet how wonderful it is to know the facts and to be able to prevent further damage, and even cancer, and look years younger—if, and only if, you stay out of the sun.

Some sun damage can be reversed by staying out of the sun and using sunscreen year-round. Sunscreens that protect against UVA and UVB rays—those which cause the most wrinkling, cancer, and sunburn—must contain one of the following ingredients: avobenzone, titanium dioxide, or zinc dioxide. It certainly doesn't hurt to use an oil-free SPF 25 on your face year-round (this is not mandatory, but is my personal preference). During the summer months, or when you are going to be out in the sun, you should use an SPF 15 (at the very least) on the rest of your body as well.

Dry Skin and Wrinkles

Dry skin does not cause wrinkles. Wrinkles appear on both dry and oily skins. They are the result of sun damage, gravity, heredity, and environmental factors. One recourse is to minimize the appearance of these wrinkles by removing dead cells and to prevent further damage. Cell renewal does not affect the collagen or elastin fibers that deteriorate from exposure to the sun and are the primary cause of wrinkles. However, the appearance of these wrinkles on all skin types can be greatly improved by exfoliating the dead skin cells.

Perhaps the greatest products to be introduced over the last several years for exfoliation have been the alpha hydroxy (AHA) and salicylic (BHA) acids. Regular use of these products offer women of all ages the chance to have smooth, clear skin. Using these products as part of your daily skin-care routine is discussed later in this chapter.

PROFESSIONAL SKIN CARE

The laundry list of experts to see gets longer each year, as does the need to take better care of yourself to remain youthful and healthy. I've added a dermatologist and plastic surgeon to my list of annual doctor visits. Although many of you may want only a simple skin-care routine and products to use at home, I urge you to also consider a yearly visit to a good dermatologist. In addition to maintaining beautiful skin, your dermatologist is your first line of defense against skin cancer, which has increased alarmingly over the last several years. Early detection saves lives, so consider your annual dermatologist checkup for moles, warts, and any suspicious skin lesions just as important as a Pap smear or mammogram.

For those of you who are serious about getting your skin in the best possible condition and following up with a good at-home skin-care routine, dermatologists and plastic surgeons offer treatments that are less extreme than surgery that are also worth considering. They are not as expensive as plastic surgery or the more invasive procedures such as liposuction, they take little or no healing time, and they offer excellent results. The only question to be considered is which treatment is best for you? Study all the options, then discuss them with your skin-care specialist to choose the right one for you.

Plastic and Cosmetic Surgery

Plastic and cosmetic surgery is a very personal choice, and one that is not right for everyone. If you are going to consider surgery, make sure that you see a board-certified physician who is willing to let you see examples of his or her work. Although plastic surgery is expensive—and is not for everyone—new techniques and procedures, such as enscopic facelifts, laser resurfacing, and liposuction, produce wonderful results with less risk and easier and shorter healing times.

Glycolic Acid Peels

Glycolic acid peels are fruit-based skin surface peels. When applied to the skin, the glycolic acid creates a slight burning or irritation, and within a few days the very top layer of skin sloughs off, leaving a smooth surface. At the same time, the irritation puffs the skin slightly, making it appear tighter and smoother. Alpha hydroxy over-the-counter treatments contain an average of 3 to 5 percent (at most 8 percent) glycolic acid. These are sufficient amounts for daily skin care; however, to get a deeper peel, 30 percent solution may be applied by trained staff in a salon, and 30 to 70 percent solutions are available from a physician.

The recommended sequence for a professional glycolic acid peel, is four to six treatments, a week apart, of increasing strengths from 30 percent to 70 percent, depending on your skin's condition and type. Your skin is cleansed thoroughly with alcohol, the glycolic acid is wiped over your face, left about

MICRODERMABRASION is a natural way to exfoliate the skin. It removes irregular skin dead cells, thus promoting cell renewal at the basal level. It also vacuums away debris and impurities that clog pores and allows the therapeutic products to evenly penetrate the skin for better results.

Dermabrasion is achieved by using aluminum oxide crystals (corundum power) to naturally exfoliate and vacuum impurities from the skin. Dermabrasion is especially successful in treating acne and acne-prone skin problems related to aging, including dyscromia, hyperpigmentation, fine lines, and moderate wrinkles. It reduces uneven pigmentation, sun damage, scarring, and stretch marks. The visible effects that can be expected are:

◆ Softening of fine lines and wrinkles

◆ Less acne, decreased breakouts, and reduction of superficial acne scars

◆ Lighter skin color

◆ Elimination of dull, rough, discolored skin due to aging

◆ Improved tone and texture

◆ More lustrous translucent skin

MICRODERMABRASION

two to three minutes, and washed off. There is some mild stinging, but you can resume work and normal activities immediately, and you can apply makeup within three hours.

Within a few days, you may experience some redness and slight peeling. Continued weekly treatments of increasing strengths, for four to six weeks, will result in noticeably smoother skin, eliminate any slight discoloration and unevenness in texture, and soften minor lines and wrinkles. Periodic single treatments throughout the year will help to maintain your new smooth skin, especially when combined with a good at-home alpha hydroxy lotion or cream as part of your regular routine.

Microdermabrasion

With new microdermabrasion treatments, known by trademarks Derma Peel™ and Power Peel™, the skin is zapped for twenty to thirty seconds with superfine aluminum oxide crystals, which lift off dead cells. Despite the comparison to sandblasting used by some practitioners, there is very little trauma, just a slight reddening of the skin following treatment. After one visit, you'll notice cleaner pores and fewer wrinkles; several treatments will reduce scars.

New Peels

Oxygen, erbium lasers, and Micro Peels™ used by qualified professionals can improve your skin and keep it looking young and clear, with little or no healing or downtime, specially if you start the treatments sooner rather than later. All these procedures are less invasive than the original dermabrasion, a procedure in which rotating wire brushes plane off layers of skin, resulting in scabbing and long healing times, or the deeper CO_2 lasers, which produce more dramatic results but require longer healing time and come with the risks associated with more extensive plastic surgery.

Plumping Up and Filling In Lines and Crevices

Smoothing the skin surface, eliminating fine lines and wrinkles, and cleaning pores are steps in skin conditioning and repair. Another trend has been to fill in the furrows that develop in the area between the eyebrows, across the forehead, and around the nose, or plumping up the lip line with a collagen like Zyderm™, or a newer non-animal hyaluronic acid like Restylane™. These substances are injected with a small needle, the procedure can be done on your lunch hour, and the treatments produce very good and immediate results. Since these substances are slowly absorbed by the body, repeat visits are necessary every three to four months. For long-term results, a more permanent filler, Gore-tex™, can be implanted.

Botox

To prevent deep lines at the bridge of the nose, around the eye area, and across the forehead, or to keep them from getting worse, many people are now resorting to injections of Botox, a poison that causes botulism, to paralyze the muscles that create these lines. Although injecting poison sounds scary, it has proven to be safe. This new cosmetic application is perhaps the most significant innovation to come along. It is now also being injected in the fine lines around the eye. The improvement is amazing, but, once again, it lasts only months and then must be readministered.

A SIMPLE, BASIC SKIN-CARE ROUTINE

After all that has been said about the new products on the market, I have found that a very simple skin-care routine works for any skin type. It begins with cleansing and toning, followed by a combination of an AHA product for exfoliation, a vitamin treatment, moisturizer, and a good sunscreen. For women over forty, a vitamin and retinol firming treatment can be added. Although the products vary for different skin types, the differences are minor. Modifications for oiliness, dryness, or sensitivity can easily be made with a change of cleanser, moisturizer, or base. Also keep in mind that your skin is constantly changing and is affected by climate and weather conditions, indoor and outdoor humidity and temperature, and

A NEW TREATMENT available at Donsuki Salon uses low-current, electro-stimulation to tone, tighten, and stimulate circulation. Treated skin is smoother and firmer and there is a significant reduction in wrinkles and loose skin. Overall improvement in skin tone and texture is the result of increased circulation in treated areas. The "instant" face and body lifts are very popular with high-profile clients who need a quick boost before an event, giving skin a significantly smoother and firmer look. This treatment is successful on both men and women.

This treatment works without causing trauma to the skin, but the results are not permanent. For maximum improvement, mainte-nance treatments are necessary. This procedure can be used on almost all areas of the body. Results vary depending on skin or body area condition. A series of treatments are needed for optimum results; however, a significant (temporary) facelift can be achieved in only one visit!

INSTANT FACE & BODY LIFT

other external factors, such as pollution. Skin that may seem normal or oily today can feel dry after a ten-hour airplane ride or hours spent in the dry heat of an office. It is important to be aware of these changes and make the necessary adaptations with your skin-care products. Let's look at a basic plan for all skin types.

Cleansers

Thorough, gentle cleansing is the most important step in any good skin care routine. I prefer water-soluble cleansers that wash off with water and leave skin feeling clean, smooth, and non-oily. Look for ones that will wash off makeup without stripping your skin of all oil, leaving it tight and dry. On the other hand, you don't want a cleanser that leaves a greasy residue.

Use cleansers with warm water and rinse thoroughly. You may need to wash a second time if you've been wearing heavy makeup or notice excess oil or perspi-ration. It is not necessary to use a cleanser with AHA or special vitamins and minerals since they will rinse off and can sting your eyes. The purpose of the cleanser is to gently clean the skin. The time to add special products is after cleansing, when they remain on the skin.

There are cleansers for dry and oily to normal skin types. For very oily skin, you may find that a stronger, more drying cleanser is preferable. Cleansers for dry skin often have more emollients. Remember that the cleanser's job is to remove makeup and dirt, so a general, all-purpose, gentle cleanser can work for all skin types, leaving the skin clean and soft. And contrary to what advertisers say, it is not necessary to buy all your skin-care products from the same company for them to work well.

Toners

The primary reason for using a non-irritating toner is to remove any traces of dirt or makeup that your cleanser may have missed. Although toners claim to reduce pores, eliminate oil, and refine skin, most do not. Oil production is hormonal, and pore size cannot be changed. You may notice that immediately after you use a toner, especially one that contains alcohol or an irritant, your pores appear smaller. This is due to a slight inflammation from the irritant, which subsides within minutes.

Although toners are often available for both dry and oily skin, a mild toner, with little or no alcohol, is good for all skin types. Some new toners contain AHA or small quantities of salicylic acid, which can clear pores and refine skin texture. I personally use an AHA and salicylic acid solution following cleansing. It seems to serve the purpose of going over the skin once again after cleansing and depositing the AHA and BHA necessary to exfoliate, unclog pores, and smooth the skin.

Exfoliants

After cleansing and toning, you may use an AHA cream for dry skin or AHA lotion or solution for oily skin. Often a beta hydroxy acid, such as salicylic acid, in a small volume (1 to 2 percent) is added to AHA products for oily skin. For very dry or sensitive skin, use a lower-percentage AHA, 3 to 5 percent; for oilier or less sensitive skin, try 5 to 8 percent. The additional BHA for oily skin unclogs the pores by exfoliating the cells within the pores, and is less irritating. BHA is often less irritating than AHA.

In addition to AHA, a Retin A or Renova™ product can also be used for exfoliation and deep cellular repair.

Vitamins and Antioxidants

Another recent entrant to skin-care lines is topically applied vitamins. There has been much controversy over the benefits. Some experts say that vitamins do little or no good since they cannot penetrate the skin. Others claim that if nothing else they provide a barrier to dehydration and work as an exfoliant and antioxidant, protecting the skin from the elements, especially the sun. Tretinoin, introduced in the market as Retin A years ago as a treatment for acne, and Renova, a newer, milder version for treating wrinkles, are derivatives of vitamin A.

Clinical tests have shown that use of Retin A and Renova affect cell growth and stimulate collagen production over time. Both treatments are approved by the U.S. Food and Drug Administration (FDA), and are available by prescription only in cream or solution to eliminate fine lines and wrinkles and restore collagen. Use of both Retin A and Renova initially causes some redness and peeling. After six to eight weeks the peeling stops, and the surface and deeper benefits continue as long as you continue to use the product.

Retinol, also a vitamin A derivative, is now used by many cosmetic companies in much lower percentages than either Retin A or Renova. It does not require a prescription and is not regulated by the FDA. Although it provides some of the same benefits as Retin A and Renova, with fewer side effects, such as redness and irritation, it may not be as effective in producing the long-term effects. Experts say that you need at least 20 percent more retinol than Retin A to get even similar results and question its use when Retin A and Renova are available. However, at this time, it is less expensive, benefits are being claimed, and many users are seeing results after only several weeks.

Kinerase™, a new lotion of furfuryladenine, a natural plant extract, has been shown to be less irritating and has the same collagen-building benefits.

Vitamin C

Vitamin C is another recommended topical vitamin promoted as an anti-aging product. My first introduction to vitamin C was through Cellex-C™. It was developed based on research by doctors at Duke University and the University of Wisconsin. The researchers claim to have developed a delivery system that allows vitamin C to penetrate the skin surface to the collagen level, maintaining collagen, preventing free-radical damage, and adding additional protection from the sun.

Recently, most skin-care companies have developed their own versions of vitamin C serum. All have different percentages of L-ascorbic acid and different delivery systems; many of them have patents pending. Some have 5 percent or less L-ascorbic acid; some have 10 to 15 percent. Bear in mind that, once exposed to the air, the potency is diluted. Most of these products come in special packaging to prevent exposure to the air and light.

At a very minimum, vitamin C lotions and creams work as antioxidants. Studies have shown that the skin looks better and that additional protection is derived from ongoing use. After months of using the highest concentration of vitamin C, I saw improvement in my skin. It was firmer, tighter, and showed overall improvement in texture. Deciding to add a vitamin C product to your skin-care routine is a personal choice. At the very minimum, you will further protect your skin against environmental damage, especially the sun. Vitamin treatments, vitamin C, or combination vitamin serums,

HEALTHY TEETH and a bright, winning smile are an important part of your appearance. Both Suki and I spend a lot of timing smiling in our work—appearing on television shows, meeting and greeting clients, conducting seminars, and hosting events—so we know how important a great smile is to one's overall image.

Teeth are a subject that we used to hear about only in a health or medical context. Today, cosmetic dentists like New York's renowned Dr. Larry Rosenthal, perform "smile makeovers" on thousands of celebrity patients. It seems that these days, no one wants to leave home without their pearly whites looking even and sparkling bright.

Perfecting Your Smile

Ask your regular dentist for advice on how to make your smile as bright and beautiful as possible. Here are two ways to perfect your smile:

Whitening—Your dentist can show you his or her own in-house tooth-whitening system, which often involves sending you home with your own custom-fitted mold and enough gel to whiten your teeth to "star status." And don't forget your regular cleaning. A general cleaning done on a more regular basis may also help brighten your teeth.

Veneers and bonding—You may also wish to learn more about porcelain veneers or cosmetic bonding from a cosmetic dental specialist. Bonding is an art form that has changed the lives and careers of many people, and is by no means restricted to the world of celebrities. The result of creative and corrective cosmetic dental work is beautiful, bright, even-looking teeth. This is yet another easy beauty alternative available to you in your adulthood, should you wish to perfect what Mother Nature gave you.

A WORD ABOUT YOUR WINNING SMILE

can also be used after exfoliation or alternated with the AHA product for additional protection and some exfoliation. Try using a vitamin product in the evening and AHA product in the morning.

Other vitamins, including B and E, are being added to many skin-care products. Like vitamin C, they are all antioxidants and offer some degree of additional protection, especially from the sun. Many new products combine several different vitamins in their antioxidant formulations. Since cosmetics are not regulated by the FDA, clinical tests are not required. However, general observations and laboratory testing have shown that these vitamin-enriched products are showing results in smoothing the skin, minimizing wrinkles, and protecting skin from further damage.

Moisturizers

Moisturizers are the most misused and misunderstood products on the market. The purpose of a moisturizer is to help the skin retain moisture, attract moisture from the air, or prevent moisture loss. Moisturizers also smooth the skin since they coat any dry areas, making the cells lie flatter and wrinkles appear less visible. Regardless of price or ingredients, moisturizers will not eliminate wrinkles or dry skin. Only exfoliation will eliminate dry, flaky skin.

A light moisturizer is all that is ever needed, even for dry skin. It is not necessary to have extra-rich moisturizers, a separate moisturizer for day, extra in your foundation, another in your sunscreen, and another for night. Heavy moisturizers and multiple layers create a sticky film that makes it more

---

A.M.

+ Cleanser

+ Toner

+ AHA product in a lotion or solution for oily or normal skin and in a cream for dry skin. Use a lower - percentage AHA for dry and sensitive skin, higher for oily. Also consider adding a BHA for oily skin.

+ Optional: Vitamin C or combination vitamin serum.

+ Sunscreen in a moisturizer base or a separate sunscreen and moisturizer. Use either oil-free or regular depending on skin type and time of year.

P.M.

+ Cleanser

+ Toner

+ AHA or Renova, Retin A or retinol product

+ Optional: Addition of Vitamin C after AHA in AM or alternate with Retin A or Renova in evening.

+ Moisturizer if needed

SKIN-CARE CHECKLIST

difficult to exfoliate the dead dry cells, even on dry skin. For very dry skin, choose a moisturizer with extra emollients, but not one that is heavy and sticky.

For those with oily skin or combination skin, a light, oil-free moisturizer is an option. However, not everyone needs moisturizer. I cannot even begin to tell you the number of times a sales clerk has tried to convince me that I absolutely need a moisturizer. Despite knowing better, I have tried many, only to reconfirm, over and over again, that I don't need anything extra on my face, especially in the summer. I occasionally use a light moisturizer around my eyes or on a dry patch that may appear, however infrequently.

Most sunscreens, even oil-free versions, are contained in a moisturizer base. It is therefore often sufficient for those with oily to normal skin to use a good sunscreen as a daily moisturizer. For those of you with oily skin, an oil-free sunscreen is a perfect moisturizer and offers protection from the sun.

Often, the only difference between nighttime and daytime moisturizers is that the nighttime moisturizer does not need to contain a sunscreen. If you choose a daytime moisturizer with a sunscreen, it may be necessary to keep a separate one for night. Some new nighttime moisturizers combine vitamin and retinol treatments and therefore are multipurpose.

Sunscreens

Since we all need sunscreens, and most sunscreens are in a moisturizer base, a good sunscreen is a "must have" to add to your daily skin-care routine. Oil-free sunscreens leave skin feeling smooth, with no sticky or oily residue, perfect for women with oily or combination skin. If you prefer a basic moisturizer, use an oil-free sunscreen with SPF of at least 15 in addition to your moisturizer. Although many foundations also contain sunscreens, check to see if the rating is SPF 15 and if it has one of the three ingredients necessary for protection: avobenzone, titanium dioxide, or zinc oxide.

Eye Cream

There is really no need for a separate eye cream unless the area around your eyes is different than the rest of your skin or is especially dry. In this case, you may want a richer eye cream or moisturizer for the eye area. Since I have oily or combination skin and use only oil-free products, I do use eye cream.

Over the years it has often been said that eye creams are different than moisturizers in that they do not attract water. It was believed that using a moisturizer around the eye attracted or retained water, resulting in puffiness in the morning. I have found that any puffiness that may result is due to some of the cream getting into the eye and irritating the surrounding tissue. More and more companies are promoting moisturizers that work for all areas of the face. Just be careful, when applying cream around the eye, not to get too close to the lash line.

An example of an all-purpose moisturizer is La Mer, a fairly heavy, expensive product that is supposed to be the only cream you'll ever need, for eyes, lips, face, and even body, regardless of skin type. It claims to have seaweed extracts that are beneficial to all skin types. I personally find it too heavy, but I know people who love it and use it as their only moisturizing product.

Masks and Scrubs

Prior to the introduction of the AHA and BHA acids, masks and scrubs were the preferred exfoliants. Many people still like the feel of a cooling or soothing mask, and the "time off" or relaxation that automatically comes with allowing the mask to set. Once again, any benefit, including tightening or reducing pores, is only temporary. And any exfoliation from the mask is not as effective as that from AHA products.

Scrubs can be very abrasive and irritating and not as effective as AHA products. Continued use of these products is a personal choice. Sometimes it's hard to make a change and eliminate a routine that makes you feel good. At least consider the alternatives and cut down on the number of products and steps in your skin-care routine. Alternatively, a mild scrub or a buff puff may help eliminate any flaky skin resulting from the peeling or lifting of dead skin cells from the AHA or BHA treatments.

Enzyme Peels

Very gentle enzyme peels offer another alternative to exfoliation that is gentle and smooths the skin surface.

Self-Tanners

Most of us still like the look of a tan. It seems to cover minor skin imperfections and impart a healthy glow. Fortunately, for those who still don't want to give up having a tan, the new self-tanners are very good—they provide nice color and coverage, and they are safe. As a rule, legs look better when a self-tanner is used year-round. It seems that with age comes those dry, chalky-looking legs. They really do look much better with a little color.

Some self-tanners are easier to use than others. Sprays go on lighter and provide a more even application, for example. Regardless of the type, brand, or cost, take care to smooth it on evenly. Use a medium or light shade and apply extra coats; this will eliminate streaking and allow you to better control the color. Some newer self-tanners contain a bronzer, which deposits color right away, allowing you to better judge the application and get instant color—a good choice when you need a quick fix.

Skin contains melanin, carotene, and hemoglobin. New research on melanin has created a product that will tan your skin in your own natural shade and provide some UVA protection. The product was expected to be introduced in the United States during the year 2000.

SUMMING UP

I hope this review of products and treatments can help you maintain a clear, smooth complexion with a minimum amount of work, time, and money. There are so many options and choices available that you could spend a fortune and months trying every new product that comes on the market. While it is important to be aware of new innovations, once you have a program that works for you, stay with it. In summary, you want to

- ✦ Cleanse, tone, exfoliate, and protect your skin.
- ✦ Stay out of the sun and use a sunscreen.
- ✦ Take care of yourself by eating right, exercising, and getting plenty of rest.
- ✦ Consult with your local salon esthetician.
- ✦ See a dermatologist once year and keep ahead of any problems that may develop.

Now that your hair looks great and your skin is clear and smooth, in the next chapter I will show you how to enhance your features and create a simple makeup color and application program, one that is appropriate for you and your lifestyle.

Modern Makeup
and More

EVERYTHING OLD IS NOT NEW AGAIN

*M*akeup colors, application techniques, and styles change with the fashions. I can often judge a woman's age by the colors of makeup she uses and the way she applies it. For some reason, we tend to get comfortable with "doing it the same way we did when we learned how." But, since you've come this far in this book, we'll assume that you are committed to change and are on your way to taking care of yourself and updating your look. Your hair is restyled and in good condition, and your complexion is smoother and clearer than it has been in years. What a great place to be. But the fun part is yet to begin. Now it is time to dress your face.

MAKEUP TIME—
LET THE FUN BEGIN

Over the last several years, more casual clothes are being worn not only for work but to upscale restaurants, even the theater. The same trends are apparent in makeup. Although there are hundreds of shades and many new products, there are some makeup basics that always look natural and complement every woman. Whether you like neutrals, pastels, or more vivid colors, there are shades and tones that will enhance your coloring and ways of applying them that will accent your best features.

Keep in mind a valuable tip from Suki. "As an experienced cosmetologist, I find that many women as they age tend to apply more makeup than they need. Rather than putting on more and more makeup to add color to their look, all they really need may be a hair-color modification and the right makeup colors to create better color balance," she says.

LET YOUR COLORING BE YOUR GUIDE

My previous books describe in detail my system for identifying colors that complement your physical characteristics. I stand by my color system and feel that everyone should understand his or her own color characteristics and use the information as the basis for color selection for not just clothing, but especially for makeup.

Putting colors on your face that look like an extension of your own coloring will provide you with the most natural and flattering results. If your objective, on the other hand, is to create an exaggerated color contrast, you now have the information to create the most extreme and effective color selection by choosing colors in the category least like your own.

To summarize the most flattering color groups for your physical characteristics, review the charts on pages 88 through 93. Remember that your personality and personal lifestyle allow you to modify your most complementary palettes to create more personalized color combinations.

✦ If your coloring is bright or deep, you will find that the bright and deep colors create balance and harmony with your stronger coloring and contrast. However, if you want a more natural look, are more conservative, or are not fond of stronger colors, soften them by mixing them with lighter or more muted shades. By softening your makeup, you will achieve a look that is more comfortable for you.

✦ If your coloring is light or muted and you prefer bright and deep colors, you will need to increase the intensity of your makeup, using care not to go so dark that your lips overpower your eyes.

◆ If your coloring is cool, be careful with foundations that are too cool or ash. Use a neutral or slightly warm tone to add a fresh, youthful glow to your complexion. For a more natural look, choose neutral shades that by definition will have some warm undertones. Avoid heavy brown tones.

◆ Warm colors can be for all. The warm colors are shades that people either love or hate. Fortunately, the earth tones can be worn successfully by many women. The neutral beige and brown tones are perfect for casual and no-makeup looks. Women with deep or muted coloring look quite striking when warm tones are combined with neutrals like black, gray, and navy for contrast. The lighter and brighter warm colors are easy for many women to wear, especially coral, coral pink, and apricot.

I will now take you step by step through makeup products, their benefits, and my personal observations. I will then recommend specific makeup colors for your characteristics and provide you with simple application techniques for each product.

A SURVEY BY *New Woman* magazine shows that age has a lot to do with which cosmetic product women feel is most important.

Twenties
Body moisturizer
Fragrance
Hairstyling products
Facial moisturizer
Eyeliner

Thirties
Body moisturizer
Hairstyling products
Fragrance
Mascara
Lipstick

Forties
Body moisturizer
Fragrance
Facial moisturizer
Mascara
Hairstyling products

Fifties
Lipstick
Body moisturizer
Fragrance
Hairstyling products
Facial moisturizer

TOP FIVE BEAUTY PRODUCTS USED BY AGE

APPLYING MAKEUP

Concealer

✦ *Apply concealer in recesses, frown lines, and wrinkles using a small brush. Blend with ring finger or sponge.*

✦ *For light shadows and lines, apply concealer over foundation. For dark shadows and lines, apply concealer under foundation, touching up any areas that need extra after foundation is applied.*

✦ *Concealer colors should be lighter than your foundation, but must be blended carefully so that you don't see "white" circles under your eye.*

Foundation and Powder

✦ *Dot foundation on nose, forehead, cheeks, and chin. Blend with fingers or damp sponge evenly over face and lips.*

✦ *Dip powder brush into loose translucent powder. Tap off excess. Apply across eye and cheek. Dust over chin area and along jawbone.*

✦ *Alternative: Use one of the new powder/foundation combinations for a natural, sheer, matte finish. Use wet for more coverage and dry for light coverage and touchups. Apply with downward strokes to smooth over any facial hairs.*

Eyebrow Pencil

✦ *To shape eyebrows, line up a pencil or brush handle alongside nose. This is where the eyebrow should begin. Pivot pencil over center of eye to find peak of your arch. Then pivot to outer corner of eye for end of brow. Fill in brows with a taupe eye shadow, applied with a small brush. Use short strokes for a more natural look.*

✦ *Alternative: Fill in brows with a pencil using short strokes and brush with an eyebrow brush until blended.*

Blush

✦ *Apply blush along top of cheekbones, beginning under center of eye, and smooth up and out into hairline. Do not bring blush lower than imaginary line from bottom of nose to just under ear, or too close to eye.*

✦ *After finishing cheeks, brush lightly across forehead, nose, and chin for a soft hint of color.*

Eyeliner

✦ *Apply along outer edge of upper lid and under lower lashes. Do not enclose entire eye. Start two-thirds or half of the way in and end at corner of eye. This will open your eye, make it look larger, and make your lashes look thicker. Use colors separately or blend two together.*

Eyeshadow

✦ *Highlighter—Cover entire lid up to brow with a neutral highlighter shadow to open eye and even out lid color.*

✦ *Contour—Use contour eyeshadow along crease of your eye to lift and enhance your orbital bone. Start under brow alongside nose and bring to outer edge of eye. Do not go to brow. Allow highlighter to accent area under brow.*

✦ *Accent—Add accent eyeshadow color on the outer third of lid in a triangular shape in an upward and outward direction. Using a small brush, apply a small amount of shadow under lower lash at outer corner.*

✦ *Blend highlighter, contour, and accent eyeshadows together with a soft brush.*

Mascara

✦ *Apply mascara to lower and upper lashes. Use comb to separate.*

Lipstick and Lip Pencil

✦ *Draw three vertical lines in center of lips with lip pencil. Use lip pencil to outline lips. Use colors to blend with or match lipstick shades. Fill in lined lips with lipstick using a lip brush.*

Makeup for Your Color Type

DEEP

Eyeshadows

Highlighter

Use neutral shades like Champagne,
Soft Peach, and Pink.

Contour and Eyeliner

Use neutral shades like Charcoal and Brown.

Accent

Use rich tones like Purple Passion,
Sea Green, and Navy.

Lipstick and Lip Pencil

Use rich tones like True Red,
Plum, and Brick.

Blush

Use darker tones like Berry and Brick

Mascara

Use Black or Brown.

Makeup for Your Color Type

LIGHT

Eyeshadows
Highlighter

Use neutral shades like Champagne, Soft Peach, and Pink.

Contour and Eyeliner

Use neutral shades like Taupe and Gray.

Accent

Use pastel tones like Turquoise, Sky Blue, and Plum.

Lipstick and Lip Pencil

Use colors like Pink, Coral, and Rose.

Blush

Use softer tones like Coral Pink and Rose.

Mascara

Use Black or Brown.

Makeup for Your Color Type

BRIGHT

Eyeshadows
Highlighter

Use neutral shades like Champagne, Soft Peach, and Pink.

Contour and Eyeliner

Use neutral shades like Taupe and Gray.

Accent

Use colors like Purple, Bright Navy, and Turquoise.

Lipstick and Lip Pencil

Use clear bright colors like Red, Berry, and Fuchsia.

Blush

Use colors like Berry and Persimmon.

Mascara

Use Black or Brown.

Makeup for Your Color Type

MUTED

Eyeshadows
Highlighter

Use neutral shades like Champagne,
Soft Peach, and Pink.

Contour and Eyeliner

Use neutral shades like Taupe and Cocoa.

Lipstick and Lip Pencil

Use brownish pink tones like Beige,
Antique Rose, and Pink Sand.

Accent

Use earthy tones like Khaki, Dusty Plum,
and Gray-Blue.

Blush

Use soft colors like Dusty Rose and Sand.

Mascara

Use Black or Brown.

Makeup for Your Color Type

WARM

Eyeshadows
Highlighter

Use neutral shades like Champagne
and Soft Peach.

Contour and Eyeliner

Use neutral tones like Honey and Khaki.

Lipstick and Lip Pencil

Use earthy red colors like Coral,
Apricot, and Brick.

Accent

Use soft colors like Dusty Plum,
Olive, and Teal.

Blush

Use warm tones like Terra Cotta and Peach.

Mascara

Use Black or Brown.

Makeup for Your Color Type

COOL

Eyeshadows
Highlighter

Use neutral shades like
Champagne and Pink.

Contour and Eyeliner

Use neutral tones like Blue-Gray and Taupe.

Lipstick and Lip Pencil

Use the rich red colors like Berry,
Dusty Rose, and Wine.

Accent

Use blues and purples like Grape,
Navy, and Periwinkle.

Blush

Use earthy shades like Mauve and Rose.

Mascara

Use Black or Brown.

CHOOSING THE RIGHT PRODUCTS FOR YOU

Foundation

Selecting the right foundation color and texture is one of the most important steps in your makeup selection and application. The right foundation color will even out your skin and provide the perfect canvas on which to apply the rest of your color. The biggest mistake when selecting foundation is choosing the wrong color—there are too many colors and too many cool foundations. If you were to ask several artists to paint swatches of realistic skin tones, they would all use some yellow in their paint mix. None would use gray, pink, or blue without yellow.

Skin contains carotene, hemoglobin, and melanin, all of which produce warm characteristics. Even though some people don't have obvious "golden" undertones, and appear more neutral, they do in fact have some warm undertones. This golden, peaches and cream or ivory glow is more obvious when we are young. As we get older, our coloring fades, as evidenced by graying or ashing of hair color, softening of eye color, and the progression of a paler, often more ash tone to the skin. The last thing that we want to do is add even more ash to our skin color by using a cool foundation. Instead, we need to add color by using a slightly warmer or neutral foundation. I have also always felt that "cool" foundations give people an ashen and dull look, like that seen in people who are ill or on medications, so I recommend neutral and warm base tones.

Over the years, I've had many arguments with color and image consultants about the need for so many cool foundations and blushes, those with blue undertones. Over the last several years, however, more and more companies and experts have confirmed my theories. Bobbi Brown offers warm foundations. Calvin Klein's new foundations are warm and neutral. Paula Begoun, in her book *Don't Go to the Cosmetics Counter Without Me,* agrees with me completely about the need to eliminate the very cool, blue-based foundations. Therefore, regardless of your color category, look for foundations that range from neutral to warm or golden and look for shades like ivory, beige, bisque, cream, buff, neutral, or brown. Avoid very peach, pink, orange, and ash tones, which appear gray.

Your foundation should match and blend into your skin. Test the color along your jawline. If you have ruddy or very pink cheeks, the right foundation will tone down the redness. In fact, an ivory or warm beige with some yellow is the best color to do this. I do not reccommend color correctors, however: adding an aqua or lavender base only adds another layer, changes the color of your foundation, and creates an unnatural look. The idea is not to change your skin color, but to match it and provide a good natural cover to even out your overall coloring. The right color foundation will do all that is necessary.

If you look for neutral and warm tones, your only question should be the correct depth. If you go too light, you'll end up with a chalky look; but going too dark will age you and the makeup will leave a line of demarcation along your jawline. Remember, *a little lighter is a younger look*.

Your foundation should be light in texture and provide sufficient coverage without being thick and obvious. I prefer liquids and use a concealer on any areas that need heavier coverage. Light creams or combination powder-foundations are also effective. Powder-foundations can be used wet as a foundation and dry as powder. A heavy matte look can be aging.

Look for oil-free formulas for normal and oily skin types, keeping in mind that some oil-free foundations often contain some silicone oil. This should not penetrate the skin and clog pores. However, look at the ingredients to be sure you are really getting an oil-free foundation. Most oil-free foundations give a light, matte look but will not prevent or absorb oil. You can use blotter paper during the day and touch up with powder to control the shine from the oil.

Oil-base foundations are best for dry skin, but avoid extra-heavy bases, which seep into any lines or creases. Use a good moisturizer and a light oil-base foundation for the most natural look. Avoid putting foundation on your neck. If the color is correct, it will blend with your neck and there will be no need to blend below the jawline. The only result of using foundation on your neck is makeup on your collar—not a pretty sight.

Concealer

Concealers, like foundations, should be neutral in tone. Avoid pink, peach, or orange shades. Use a beige shade that is one to two shades lighter than your foundation. Concealers should be thicker and provide more coverage than your foundation. They are primarily for dark circles under the eyes, or for lines and areas that need extra coverage.

Liquid concealers, or those that are applied with a sponge at the end of a wand, do not cover as well as creams. If they are too oily, they seep into lines and do not stay put. A light application of Dermablend™, a thick coverup that is made to camouflage scars and birthmarks, mixed with a little moisturizer, often works well on deep circles and discoloration. Some people find it drying, but I have been very satisfied with the coverage and find it stays all day.

IF YOU PREFER A PENCIL, it is important to work with a sharp point and to use short, feathered strokes. It often helps to use two colors, mixing them for a more natural look. After applying color, brush over the brow with a toothbrush or special eyebrow brush to thoroughly blend the color.

EYEBROW TIP

Remember that light brings features forward, and dark makes them appear to recede. To bring dark circles forward and make them appear less deep, put concealer only on the dark areas or creases, avoiding any puffy area around the circle. Applying a small amount of concealer with a thin brush along nasal folds and along the lip line will make these lines less obvious. I also use concealer to cover small broken blood vessels along the side of my nose and chin.

Using concealer to cover a pimple or breakout may cause additional irritation due to the oil in the concealer. There are special coverups for blemishes, but foundation usually covers these spots effectively. Getting too much of a buildup, by applying layers of coverup, only makes the spot more obvious. Instead, you need only touch up the problem areas and apply a light coat of foundation and powder.

Powder

Powder choices include loose, pressed, and the new wet/dry powder foundation combinations. Loose powder is preferred by most makeup artists, because it provides the lightest coat and sets the foundation. It also provides a smooth surface on which to apply blush. Without powder, the foundation often grabs the blush and prevents smooth application. Loose powder is also suggested for oily skin, because it contains no oils or waxes, which are contained in pressed powder.

Pressed powder is easier to use and provides more coverage. It is especially convenient for touchups in the afternoon or on the go, since loose powder can be very messy to carry around. The dual-finish powders and combination powder-foundations provide maximum coverage when used dry. If you want additional coverage for evening or special occasions, use dual powder over foundation. I also find that these dual powders used alone, without foundation, over my sunscreen, give me enough coverage with fewer layers, in humid weather or when I want to use as little makeup as possible.

Choose a shade of powder that is the same shade as or as similar to your foundation as possible. Avoid dark shades and bronzing colors that streak and look unnatural. Ivory, neutral, and yellow powders add softness and tone down any redness or ruddiness. Always apply any powder with a large brush to get the lightest and most even application.

If you want a tanned or bronzed look, use the loose bronzing powder with a big brush, in much the same way you would use blush. Brush along the top of your cheeks, across your forehead, and on your nose and chin. These are the areas that the sun hits first, and applying color there will make your bronzing look more realistic.

Blush

Makeup artists differ on when to apply blush. Many prefer to put it on after the eyes are made up to better judge the amount necessary to balance the eye makeup. I like to apply blush as soon as possible because a little color makes me look better and gives me a basis for beginning my eye makeup. When I'm finished with my shadow and lipstick, just a touch more blush or brushing over the original application with another light coat of loose powder is all that's needed.

While I have emphasized the need for neutral and warm foundations, I don't feel the same way about blush colors. Often the brown, beige, and sand colors do not add enough color or brightness to the cheek, but create a dark, bruised effect. Soft shades—peach, soft pink, rose, plum, and tawny colors—in powder blushes and matte finishes look more natural. The frosted or iridescent shades settle in lines and wrinkles, so it's best to save them for evening. A touch of iridescence along the top of the cheekbone makes a great evening look.

Always use a large brush and apply blush on the cheekbone, but avoid getting too close to the eye or nose. With what is left on the brush, brush along your forehead, down the nose, and across your chin.

Eyebrows

Eyebrows frame and enhance your eyes. For some reason eyebrows are often ignored in the total makeup-application process. Most people tweeze a few hairs that seem to fall outside their natural line, and unless they have no brows or very light brows, they just move on to eyeshadow.

The most important aspect is to get the right shape and length. Hold a pencil or brush handle vertically at the outer edge of your nose. Your eyebrow should start directly above the outer edge of your nostril. Now hold the pencil from the outer edge of your nostril diagonally to the outer edge of your eye. Your eyebrow should end where the diagonal line of the pencil crosses your brow line. Your brow should arch right above the outer edge of the iris of your eye.

Tweezing the stray hairs that are outside this area is a first step. Filling in any sparse areas or darkening the brow itself is the tricky part. Use a neutral shade of powder; for example, you can use the same taupe eyeshadow that you use for a contour shadow. Apply it with a stiff angled brow brush. Suki suggests that, to ensure the perfect shape, your cosmetologist or stylist should create the right eyebrow shape for your eye and face.

Eyeliner

Eyeliner is one of the most important steps in eye makeup. I would rather skip eyeshadow or even foundation than eliminate eyeliner. The purpose of eyeliner is to make the eyes look bigger and lashes look thicker. There are many different eyeliners, a number of which look unnatural and exaggerated. Liquid liners, for example, tend to be difficult to use and do not create the most natural effect. A better option is to use a neutral-colored pencil or powder, drawing the line just along the upper and lower lash line. The line length will depend on your eyelid size and shape.

Before lining my eye, I like to use an eyeshadow base. Foundation works well for those who use an oil-base foundation. If you use an oil-free base, I recommend priming the lid with a cream shadow base, since eyelids do not have many oil glands. It keeps the lid soft and helps the eyeshadow to remain on all day.

Use eyeliner prior to putting on eyeshadow. By putting the liner on first, you can then brush a neutral base coat of shadow over the line, softening it and correcting any section that needs to be evened or smoothed out. Use a stiff, flat, square brush. Dip the brush into a deep neutral shadow and gently place it along your upper and lower lash lines, moving it over the exact area you want to cover. You can also use a soft eyeliner pencil.

Eyeshadow

Eyeshadow seems to be the most difficult type of makeup to apply, and poorly applied, it can ruin an otherwise nice look. For some reason, too much color is an all too common mistake. Eyeshadow should do exactly what the name says, shadow the eye, making the color brighter, accenting your bone structure, or camouflaging any minor imperfections. The purpose is not to see how much color you can put on the lid. The illustrations on pages 100 through 102 show how to modify your eye makeup for different eye shapes, such as deep-set, prominent, and wide-set.

I recommend only neutral shades of eyeshadow, except for an accent color at the outer edge or as a touch to accent the liner. I also like matte-finish powders and those with a slight sheen. I have never found a cream that looks natural. Creams tend to be harder to apply and blend with other shades. Look for powders that go on smoothly and have enough pigment to last all day or evening and allow for blending.

Iridescent and frosted shadows look unnatural and settle in the creases, making the lid look crepey. The only time to use eyeshadow with a little frost is evening or for a dramatic look, and then it should be placed only subtly on the center of the eyelid or on the orbital bone to create a hint of shimmer. I use a single frosted gold shadow on the top of my cheekbone and a touch on the center of my eyelid for evenings.

Mascara

Some people feel that mascara is the most essential of all cosmetics and wouldn't think of going out without it. It is a toss-up for me whether eyeliner or mascara is my first priority. There are many price ranges of mascara, and this is one product where price does not seem to make a big difference.

Neutral colors like brown, black, and brown-black are preferred choices for the most natural looks. Those that have fibers incorporated for lash lengthening cause problems, especially for contact-lens wearers, and they tend to clump more. There are both pros and cons to waterproof and regular mascara. Some women find that waterproof mascaras are more drying and harder to remove, causing lashes to pull out or break. I often use waterproof mascara, however, especially in humid weather. I find that despite my oily skin, it does not streak or leave smudges under my eyes. When wearing waterproof mascara, do first apply a lash conditioner. It protects your lashes, allows you to wash off the mascara more easily, and builds an extra coating, making your lashes appear longer

To Curl or Not to Curl

I personally always curl my lashes before applying lash conditioner or mascara. I see a big difference: curled lashes seem to open the eyes more. I have even tried the heated lash curlers and find that they curl faster. Curling your lashes is a personal choice, but do try it. Curl your lashes before applying mascara, never after, because the lashes will stick to the rubber insert and are apt to pull out.

Lipstick and Lip Pencil

A lip pencil is essential to creating a perfect lip line and lipstick application. It becomes more and more important the older we get. As we age our lip line is less well defined, there are more vertical wrinkle lines, and lipstick tends to bleed more. By using a lip pencil in the same or similar color as your lipstick, you have a crisp line and defined area for applying lipstick.

It is important to line your lip precisely along the lip line. However, it is okay to extend the lip line ever so slightly if your lips are very narrow, or to line them just inside the lip line if your lips are too full. I especially like to extend my lip line at the very center of my bottom lip, just a tiny bit. By extend, I mean draw a little more liner in the center of the outer edge, not a real extension.

In choosing lipstick, it is important to select colors within your complementary color range. It is then possible to brighten, deepen, or lighten slightly to create the look you want. Keep your lipstick and blush in the same tones.

Lipstick comes in so many different textures that it is often hard to decide what to buy. Sheers are nothing more than lip glosses; they don't last very long, and are better for the young. The matte and long-lasting versions do stay on, but are very drying. Although I like some matte foundations, eyeshadows, and blushes, matte lipsticks are aging. The creamy finishes look younger and more natural.

The question always remains: How do you keep lipstick on all day and prevent the lipstick smudge on your glass or cup? Applying one coat, powdering over, and then applying another coat helps. Filling in the entire lip with lip pencil first, then applying lipstick on top will also help. A lip sealer, like Lip Elegance™, can be applied after lipstick is blotted. A lip gloss or cream is needed to prevent drying, but lipstick stays on all day. Lip Elegance is a pure botanical product that has been used in Europe for more than fifty years. I first found it at Harrod's Department Store in London. New lip stains also stay on longer, but need a top coat of gloss to prevent drying.

- ✦ Moisten a cotton ball with a mild toner and wipe forehead, nose, and chin areas.
- ✦ Remove any lipstick.
- ✦ Freshen nose, forehead, chin, and lips with foundation.
- ✦ Dust with translucent or iridescent powder.
- ✦ Freshen eyelids with highlighter, add a little gold shadow to the center of the lids, and touch up accent color.
- ✦ Add a lighter shade of blush to top of cheekbones, and accent hollows of cheeks with deeper tone.
- ✦ Reapply lipstick and touch lip gloss or lighter shade of lipstick to center of bottom lip for a sensual look.
- ✦ Add a second coat of "color" mascara.

EVENING MAKEUP TIPS

EYE MAKEUP APPLICATION

Small

To open eyes be sure to have well-arched eyebrows. Line upper lid, gradually thickening line over the pupil. Use very thin line under lower lash from center out only. Apply a light shadow from lash line to brow. Use a darker neutral in eyelid crease, extending up and out to the orbital bone. Add accent color on outer edge of lid, extending it out and up slightly.

Wide-Set

Attract attention inward. Start brow line slightly closer to nose; arch over center of the eye, stopping slightly short of outer ending point. Line both upper and lower lash lines, starting close to corner of eye. Apply light shadow to outer half of lid, extending up to brow bone. Use darker neutral on inner corner of upper lid, extending over center of eye to blend with lighter shade. Use accent color in center of lid, blending all shades well.

Deep-Set

To make eyes appear more open, be sure to have well-arched brows, keeping as much space as possible between lid and brow. Use a very thin liner as close to the lash line as possible, starting at center of lid. Be sure to smudge so that starting point is not noticeable. Apply light shadow on entire lid, extending to brow bone. Use a darker neutral in crease. Do not extend upward. Add accent color at outer edge, extending slightly upward.

Down-Slanted

*To draw attention in an upward direction, lifting the eye, use a light shade to cover lid
and extend to brow line. Apply a darker neutral color in the crease, extending up to the orbital
bone in an upward and outward direction. Add an accent color at the outer corner of lower
and upper lid, brushing it upward in a triangular shape.*

Prominent

*To make eyes look less protruding, apply a thick line along entire upper and lower lashes.
Apply a medium to dark neutral shade over entire eyelid, extending to crease.
Emphasize crease with a slightly darker shade. Add a light neutral under brow from arch
to outer edge. Add an accent color, blending well.*

Droopy Upper Lid

*To lift eye, line lower third of lash line with fine line. Cover entire lid up to brow with
a light neutral. Accent crease by using a dark neutral in crease of eye.
Add an accent color at the outer edge of lower and upper lid, extending up and out slightly.*

Close-Set

*To make eyes appear farther apart, start brows slightly out from corner of the eye,
arch beyond the center of the pupil, and end slightly beyond corner of eye. Line outer two-thirds
of both upper and lower lash lines. Apply a light shadow over half of lid,
starting as close to inner corner as possible, and brush up to brow bone.
Cover remaining lid with a deeper neutral extending up and out. Add an accent color to the outer
third of the upper lid, brushing upward and outward, slightly beyond outer corner of the eye.*

Turned-Up

*To draw attention upward at the inner corner of the eye, line outer half of both upper
and lower lashes. Use a light shadow on inner corner of eye and under brow.
Apply darker neutral in crease and on outer half of lid.
Use accent color under lower lash line and at corner of upper lid.*

Round

*To make eyes appear more almond-shaped, avoid extremely arched brows. Line upper and lower
lid from center of lid out to the corner. Make sure that the starting point is subtly blended.
Apply light shadow over lid, extending to brow bone. Apply a darker neutral in crease of eye,
starting above the iris and extending up and out. Add accent color on outer edge of top lid again,
bringing it up and out, slightly past the outer edge of eye.*

LIPSTICK AND LIP PENCIL APPLICATION

Small

Focus attention on outer corners to make lips appear wider.
Line lip, making the line a little darker and thicker at the outer edges,
extending the line ever so slightly in the corner. Apply lipstick in the same shade as the liner,
then apply a lighter shade or gloss in the center of the upper and lower lip.

Thin or Receding Lower Lip

Line lips, making the line a little darker and thicker along the center of the bottom lip.
Fill in with lipstick the same shade as the liner.
Use a lighter shade over the bottom lip to lighten primary color slightly.
Lightening the thinner lip will make it appear thicker and fuller.

Turned Down

Line upper lip, stopping just short of outer corner.
Line lower lip, extending the line to the outer corner and feathering in slightly.
Fill in with the same shade lipstick. Apply a lighter shade over the center of the upper lip,
blending outward and allowing darker shade to remain at corners.

Wide

Line lips following natural line, but stopping just short of corners of both upper and lower lip.
Fill in with lipstick in the same or similar shade, concentrating color in the center of the lips.
Lighten slightly at outer edges.

Thin

Line lips at the outer edge of lip line, extending line ever so slightly.
Accent center of lips with darker and heavier line in the center of upper and lower lips
and at peaks of upper lip. Fill in with shade that is the same as or similar to the liner.
Use a lighter shade or gloss in the center of upper and lower lip.

Uneven

Line lips, making line on thinner side a little thicker and darker.
Fill in with lipstick the same or similar shade as the liner, but go a little darker
on the fuller side. Alternatively, fill in with the same color,
lightening the thinner half with a lighter shade or some gloss.

DIFFERENT FACES FOR DIFFERENT OCCASIONS

Natural or play

Daytime

Evening

Appendices

THE ALWAYS IN STYLE TRENDS MAGAZINE

Each week new products and services are introduced by the fashion and beauty industries. To ensure that you look and feel your best and to save you the time and effort necessary to edit through the dozens of magazines, journals, and web sites, we at Always In Style publish the online Always In Style *Trends Magazine* for your convenience. Each week there are ten new articles highlighting trends in fashion, beauty, and home decorating.

In this section you will find a sampling of the Beauty articles. I'm sure you will find the information a helpful addition to the material found in *The Essential Guide to Hair, Makeup & Skin Care*. Do visit **www.alwaysinstyle.com** for more news. You can also get personal advice by filling out the Personal Profile questionnaires on the web site or the printed version at the end of this book.

Always In Style *Trends Magazine*
Editor: Debra Scott
Publisher: Sylvia Ledesma

EYELASH BATTING 101

If you're blessed with full, long lashes with a natural curl, read no further. For the rest of us, there are, well, lashings of ways to improve those lid ornaments we unashamedly flutter (or should, anyway) to charm the opposite sex. Set curl with a **lash curler,** then apply **mascara.** For full lashes, apply a coat, brush on loose powder, then apply a second coat. Don't forget to **comb** lashes between coats to prevent clumping. Or use a **lash conditioner,** a clear base coat that conditions and thickens the lashes, before applying mascara. **False eyelashes** aren't only for Tammy Faye Bakker. In a nod to the Beatles era, fashionable women from SoHo to Seattle are applying **single lashes, flares** (sets of four), and **full lash sets** with dramatic results. Not just for special occasions, synthetic lashes look amazingly natural by day too. Just dab the root in glue and place on lid above lashes for a sex-kittenish "cat's-eye" look.

Look For:

Eyelash curling system

Lash thickener

Eyelash comb

False eyelashes (single, flares, or full sets)

Lash conditioner

LIP GUNK

From Brandy to Britney, glam girls are putting their glossiest lips forward. Get ready to make your lips shine too with the latest in lip-smacking trends. Tinted lip glosses are the mouth paint of the moment. They come in hip hues like the Gap's Tangy Cherry Lipshine and Cover Girl's Hint of Pink Shimmer Lipslick. For an almost-wet look, where only the bloom of your own lips shows through, go for a clear gloss like MAC's original Lipglass. If a gorgeous gleam isn't enough, pucker up with flavor! You'll lick your lips just *hearing* about the fab flavors available in the latest lip gunk. Bonne Bell offers eight yummy tastes, including grape and peach, in their Lip Burst line, and Liquid Love's lip glosses come in even more! The perfect pout has come a long way since Vaseline (though that old friend still does the trick if you don't mind the smell). Now all you need is someone to smooch.

Look For:

Daring flavors

Pastel glosses

Glimmer and shimmer

FAKING IT

Unlike many cancers, skin cancer can be avoided... by staying out of the sun. Exposure to UV radiation (made more prevalent by holes in the ozone layer) is the number-one melanoma-causing culprit. Even the lightest tan is a sign of skin damage and will eventually show up as wrinkled, blemished, and sagging flesh. Applying a "sunless tanning lotion" needn't result in an orange, streaky "tan." Today's sophisticated fake tan potions have been formulated to smooth on evenly in gold (for light-skinned men and women) or bronze (for darker-skinned men and women) shades that bespeak a healthy glow. Since self-tanning formulas look best on freshly buffed and moisturized skin, consider getting a kit that includes an exfoliator and moisturizer. Mechanical scrubs such as washcloths, loofahs, a rock salt and oil mixture, or pumice stones can polish away dry, rough skin, especially on knees, elbows, and ankles. Apply a moisturizer where you intend to apply the tanning lotion, and wait a few minutes while your skin drinks it up. Apply tanning cream (or spray or whatever) with the palm of your hand (not fingertips) for the most even effect. Since a fake tan usually takes between three and five hours to appear, you might do it before going to bed—but wait at least a half hour so it will be absorbed by your skin rather than your sheets. Reapply every three days. Many tans-in-a-bottle also contain tinted moisturizers that make application easy (since you can see where it's going) and give you a radiant glow while-you-wait. You can still go in the sun if you want to—many fake tan products contain sun protection. Oh yeah, did I mention that the cast of *Baywatch* used a product called Au Courant to fake their tans?

Tip: Wait at least ten minutes after applying so as not to stain your clothes. And don't forget to wash your hands immediately afterwards if you don't want to give away your secret.

Look For:

Rich moisturizers like aloe vera and natural herbs

Vitamin-based products

BRUSH STROKES

When it comes to applying makeup, every woman is an artist. Trouble is, most of us focus more on our palette than we do on the other crucial tools of the trade—the brushes. That's because we're not really sure how to use them. And it's no wonder. According to model-turned-makeup-mogul Stacey Schieffelin, we were never taught the fine art of painting our faces. With her thorough line of professional makeup brushes, Schieffelin plans to change that. "You need professional tools for professional results," says the Models Prefer proprietor. And, okay, who doesn't want to look like Cindy or Heidi? In a clever move, the Models Prefer brushes are double-ended. As Schieffelin says, "Why carry ten when you only need five?" These carefully engineered tools easily pick up product and glide it accurately onto the skin. The set includes a pointy **Lip Liner,** a square **Chisel Deluxe Fluff** for blending eye shadow, a slanted **Concealer Brush** (also useful for dabbing blemishes and highlighting brow bones), a flat **Detail Fluff Brush** for precision lining, a **Fluff Brush** for shading and contouring small areas such as the nose (to change its shape!), a **Sponge Tip Wand** to smooth color onto the eye, a **Loose Powder Brush** for allover dusting, a domed **Blush Brush** for even dispersion of powder and a **3-in-1 Eyelash Curler, Lash Comb,** and **Eyebrow Comb.** If you want to blend your makeup like an expert, brushes are a critical investment.

Mascara Tip: Use a zigzag motion at your lash roots, then sweep mascara outward and upward to prevent clumping and create a thick lash look. Models apply several thin coats rather than one thick one.

ARTFUL BROWS

If you thought that mousse and gel were only for the hair on your head, think again. These essential grooming products are the latest weapons in the savvy woman's arsenal for making her eyebrows lustrous while keeping them under control. According to Cosmetics Plus beauty expert Ingrid Pascual, the new brow look is "as natural as possible." Not too full, not too thin. But beware: brows must be very well groomed. "One hair out of place is enough to keep your face from looking fresh and clean," she says. For artistically styled brows, eyebrow kits—which contain such items as tweezers, revolutionary eyebrow "fixers" to make color stay all day, definer brushes, and even a "silhouette mold" to help you paint your brows in exactly the right place—will make a Michelangelo out of you.

Latest Products:

Eyebrow kits

Fixing shine

Eyebrow gel

Battery-operated shapers

CUTTING EDGE BRONZER

Literally "cutting edge" is the new "Grater" Bronzer developed at cosmetics company Models Prefer. When you twist the cap of the innovative compact, hidden blades actually freshly "shave" off just the right amount of micro-fine, pressed bronzing powder. Thus, you can control exactly the amount of silky powder to dust onto your brush so that you can get either a light veil of color or a more vibrant bloom. The special "puff brush" that comes with the bronzer is designed to scoop up the freshly milled color to deliver a soft fairy dusting of even, sun-kissed color. The brains and beauty behind the line of high-quality cosmetics is stunning former model Stacey Schieffelin, who starts her beauty program on QVC with a bare, unmade-up face... then proceeds to paint it throughout the duration of the show. The makeup mogul includes highly informative "tips of the trade" with each beauty product. When it comes to bronzer, the vivacious blonde advises applying it from the outer part of the face and moving toward the center. By starting at the cheek, she warns, you'll deposit a splotch of color on the front of your face creating a "clownlike" effect. "Always use circular movements with your brush," she says. This way the bronzer is "raised to the areas of the face where the sun would naturally hit: cheekbones, crest of nose, brow bones, temples, chin, jawline, and neck." To make long faces appear wider, she recommends applying bronzer horizontally at the cheekbones. Short or round faces, she says, can be lengthened by applying bronzer in a triangular pattern blended toward the temples.

RAY WATCH—
THE ABCs OF SPFs

As summer approaches, leave the oil for cooking and bathe your bod in sunscreen. According to Vincent DeLeo, M.D., chairman of dermatology at New York's St. Luke Roosevelt Hospital, year-round exposure to the sun can lead to brown spots, uneven coloring, sallowness, sagging, wrinkling, rosacia (whatever that is!) and pre-cancers—yech! But even when everything we read about the sun says bad, bad, bad, we still know the sun's rays feel good, good, good. So if you're not the type to hibernate all year (who is?), power up on protection when taking in the rays each day. The three little letters to look for are SPF which stand for "Sun Protection Factor." SPF is a ratings system that measures a sunscreen's effectiveness in protecting against harmful UVB rays. The number following the SPF describes the amount of time you can spend in the sun without burning. For example, choosing SPF 15 allows you to hang in the sun fifteen times longer than you would with no protection—without burning. Even beauty brands are pumping protection into fun products from lip gloss to moisturizer to hair care (you don't want your lovely locks to get scorched, do you?). As for the tan, many of our fave brands offering the SPF also make self-tanners! Yesss!

Check Out:

For Hair: Banana Boat Hair and Scalp Protector SPF 15

For Lips: Bobbi Brown SPF 15 lip balm
                   L'Oreal HydraSoft lipstick SPF 12

For Face: Clinique Super City Block Daily Face Protector SPF 25
                   Cover Girl Fresh Look makeup (oil-free) SPF 15
                   Maybelline Express makeup—3 in 1 (oil-free) SPF 15

Moisturizer: Neutrogena non-comedogenic facial moisturizer SPF 15
                   Biore hydrating moisturizer SPF 6

IN THE RED

Red—as in the color favored for lips, cheeks, and nails by sirens of the silver screen—is back with a vengeance. But this time around, the look has been toned down to a more subtle, modern rendition. "Movie stars had very painted mouths," says New York makeup artist Carmindy Boyer, spokesperson for Beautiful by Nature, a cosmetics line from Bath & Body Works. "Now we're seeing lip stains as opposed to lipsticks." Lipsticks, she explains, are comprised of heavy pigments that lie on top of lips—in red they are potentially overpowering and also have a tendency to bleed. Lip stains, on the other hand, are sheer colors that permeate the lips—a subtler, less messy approach to high glamour. She recommends Beautiful by Nature's red grape and apple colors. "Blondes should stick to cool reds, brunettes to true reds, and redheads to tomato reds." One of her favorite tricks is to blend lipstick on cheeks "for glow." Finish off with red nails, she advises, but keep the rest of the face bare—just a dusting of shimmer on the eyes. "With red lips you don't want heavy eyes," says the artist, who has painted the faces of models from Heidi Klum to Cindy Crawford. "You want to be able to focus on one feature at a time."

Look For:
Lipstick kits containing a spectrum of reds
Shimmering nail polishes
Lip stains

THE LIGHT STUFF

The buzz in the beauty industry is about the latest breakthrough: light-reflecting potions. Seven years in the making, Prescriptives Magic was recently launched to great fanfare. Neither makeup nor skin care, the newfangled line (which includes six products) is a kind of smoke-and-mirrors approach to beauty. Developed to manipulate light, it actually tricks the eye into thinking you have picture-perfect skin. According to Sandi, a forty-seven-year-old Californian who sits on the Cosmetic Connection Product Panel, the products feel magical when they touch the skin—even the powder feels wet and cold. Well, here she is in her own words: "It's like nothing I've ever seen before," she said on Heather Kleinman's Cosmetic Connection™ (www.cosmeticconnection.com). "I have a very ruddy and scarred complexion; Magic magically toned down the redness, evened out the color, and my face appeared smoother. Not smooth, but smoother. I felt okay about wearing Magic out of the house without foundation and I rarely go out without foundation. I felt as comfortable about how my face looked as when I am wearing foundation. I think it's great for days off or for around the house or going to work out. It truly doesn't look like you are wearing any makeup, yet it makes you look good."

The line includes Illuminating Liquid Potion, Illuminating Cream Potion, Liquid Powder, Cooling Wand, Cooling Globe, and Invisible Line Smoother. Other light reflecting products on the market include BeneFit High Beam, Estee Lauder Spotlight Skin Tone Perfector, Ultima II Glowtion, and the special recommendation of Cosmetics Plus spokesperson Ingrid Pascual, Pia Jabe Tint & Protect. "It has the benefits of a moisturizer, the protection of SPF, and an allover shimmer," she says. Our vote goes to Models Prefer Hands-Free Light Diffusing Formula which contains a revolutionary coated pigment and hundreds of tiny light-reflective particles that bounce light away from the skin. We're ready for our close-up!

YOU GO, CURL!

The slick coif that Jennifer Anniston launched a few years ago with a few strategic tosses of her mane, is finally on the wane. Not that we're returning to Nicole Kidman-esque corkscrew curls. (Have you noticed that even she's finally abandoned her natural crowning glory?) It's time to salute the waves.

"After seasons spent blowing hair straight, summer styles will be accentuating the natural wave in hair or creating curl if there isn't any," says Cody Kusakabe, director of styling at Gavert Atelier in Beverly Hills.

The perfect solution is a light body wave. If your hair is stick straight, get your rollers out of storage or try one of the ingenious methods being used by trendy stylists.

Wrap hair around rectangles of cardboard and attached with hair clips.
Wind folds of hair around long pieces of aluminum foil, fastening the ends.
Twist strands around sponge-rubber ties and roll up to your scalp.
Wrap hair around long paper towel "rollers."

For all methods, start with dry hair and add a volumizing fixative, holding tonic, styling spray, or thickening spray before and after curling. Finger-comb when dry. For curly hair, Kusakabe advises using Move Magic, an anti-frizz styling balm that makes hair "piecey."

Look For:
Volumizing fixative
Holding tonic
Styling spray
Alcohol-free products
Body-giving shampoo and conditioners
Curling brush or iron
Steam hair rollers

ARTIFICIALLY NATURAL

Nails used to be long, square, and big. The latest trend, according to Lauren Breese manager of new product development at nail enhancement company OPI, is for shorter and rounder—in other words, more natural looking nails. But that doesn't mean you can't use artificial means to achieve a natural look. The new lighter and more flexible gels are "sculpted" onto the nail to make them longer. Virtually weightless, they're less likely to break than natural nails. These translucent gels allow natural skin tone shows through. "For those who are hard on their nails, acrylic overlays are generally even stronger than gels, thus less likely to break for women who insist on using their nails as kitchen or garden tools," laughs Breese. Both gels and acrylics can be sculpted to create a "permanent French manicure" effect (white nail tip, pink nail bed). With no polish to chip off, your manicure will last for weeks. The nail shape of the moment is "squoval"—square made to look natural with rounded edges. The best natural colors are translucent whites and pinks. Of course, color is still in and looks great on the shorter nail length. Though creating a natural look may be more challenging than any guy could imagine, it's an essential part of your beauty routine. As Breese says, "Keeping your nails groomed is as important to a pulled together look as your hair, makeup or accessories."

Do you have the new nail length?

Your "free edge"—the part of your fingernail that goes from fingertip to end—should be no longer than half your nail bed—the part that goes from cuticle to fingertip. In other words a ratio of $2/3$ (nail bed) to $1/3$ (free edge).

TRIPLE ACTION

Since the new woman is a pro at driving, talking on the phone and styling her hair—all at the same time, it's a no-brainer that she wants her makeup to accomplish as many tasks as she does. Cosmetics companies are responding by creating products that pack the maximum beautifying punch. Combining skin care components with cosmetic enhancement, cuts a couple of steps out of our beauty routine. (Hooray!) This spring Helena Rubinstein introduces a foundation that not only covers blemishes and evens out skin tones—the superficial role of all foundations—but also probes deeper to lift, smooth and hydrate the face. Nu Skin has formulated their Undeviating™ Lipstick with fabulous pigment along with hydrating agents to keep lips smooth and an SPF of 15. Lipscape from AWAKE, is a creamy color that can also be applied to eyes and cheeks. What'll they think of next?

Look For:

Two-in-one or three-in-one-products
(like a foundation/powder/ moisturizer)

Anti-aging components with makeup

Waterproof and SPF features

Always In Style®

DISCOVER YOUR PERSONAL STYLE

Personal Profile Questionnaire

*D*ear friend: I hope you've enjoyed reading *The Essential Guide to Hair, Makeup & Skin Care*—now I want to help you with some free personalized style analysis and advice.

The next five pages contain printed versions of the *Always In Style Personal Profile Application* for color, body-line, skin, and hair. Simply fill out one or any combination of the profiles and return, along with a $5 check or money order for shipping and handling, to:

> Always In Style
> 1500 Harbor Boulevard
> Weehawken, NJ 07087

You will receive your Personal Profile Report, with a personalized style analysis and advice, along with a FREE* *Always In Style Seasonal Fashion Forecast*, in two to three weeks. Or, you can go to www.alwaysinstyle.com to get your analysis directly online.

I look forward to receiving your completed form, and assure you it will be held in the strictest confidence.

Doris Pooser
President and CEO
Always In Style

Money-Back Guarantee.
If you are not completely satisfied with *Doris Pooser's Makeover by Mail*, return with an explanation for a full refund.

*Retail value $15.

Please fill out the information below
and return with your completed profiles.

| MAILING AND |
| ADDITIONAL INFORMATION |

Name _____

Address _____

_____

State _____ Zip _____

Telephone: (H) (____)_____

(W) (____)_____

E-mail: _____

Color Analysis

EYE COLOR

Select the image closest to your eye color.

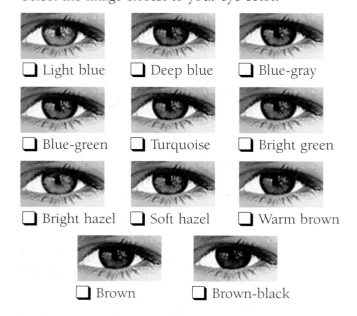

☐ Light blue   ☐ Deep blue   ☐ Blue-gray

☐ Blue-green   ☐ Turquoise   ☐ Bright green

☐ Bright hazel   ☐ Soft hazel   ☐ Warm brown

☐ Brown   ☐ Brown-black

HAIR COLOR

Select the image closest to your hair color.

☐ Silver-gray   ☐ Warm gray   ☐ Salt and pepper

☐ Light ash blonde   ☐ Medium to dark ash blonde   ☐ Light blonde

☐ Golden-blonde   ☐ Medium to dark warm blonde   ☐ Strawberry-blonde

☐ Auburn   ☐ Medium dark brown   ☐ Dark brown-black

LIPSTICK

Select the color you wear most often for lipstick.

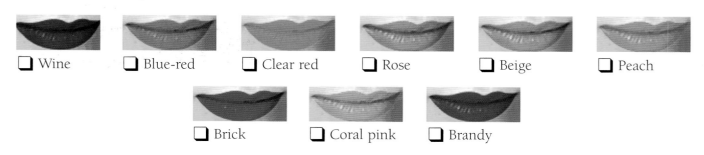

☐ Wine   ☐ Blue-red   ☐ Clear red   ☐ Rose   ☐ Beige   ☐ Peach

☐ Brick   ☐ Coral pink   ☐ Brandy

Color Analysis

Which best describes your makeup preferences?

☐ I wear makeup every day.   ☐ I wear makeup several times a week.

☐ I rarely wear makeup.   ☐ I never wear makeup.

SKIN COLOR

Select the skin-tone characteristics that best describe your skin color.

Depth

☐ Light   ☐ Medium   ☐ Olive   ☐ Dark

Freckles

☐ Freckles   ☐ no Freckles

Undertone

☐ Golden   ☐ Rose   ☐ Neutral

COLOR GROUPS

Select three color groups you like wearing according to preferences (1st, 2nd, 3rd).

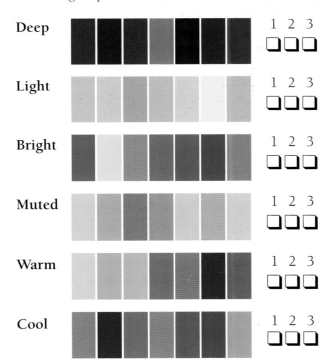

Bodyline Analysis

MEASUREMENTS

Accurate measurements assist in a correct analysis.

Height:_____ feet _____ inches

Weight:_____ pounds

Bust:_____ inches

Rib cage:_____ inches

Waist:_____ inches

Hips:_____ inches

Check one: ❏ I have a visible waist

❏ I have little or no waist

Visible   NonVisible

FIGURE CONCERNS

Please indicate if you would like helpful suggestions on any of the following:

❏ Long neck   ❏ Large hips

❏ Short neck   ❏ Narrow hips

❏ Broad shoulders   ❏ Tall (5'9" or higher)

❏ Narrow shoulders   ❏ Petite (5'2" and under)

❏ Large bust   ❏ Short legs

❏ Small bust   ❏ Long legs

❏ Long waist

❏ Short waist

FACE SHAPE

Select the shape that best describes your face.

 ❏ Square

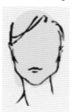 ❏ Rectangle

 ❏ Diamond

 ❏ Triangle

 ❏ Round

 ❏ Oval

 ❏ Heart

 ❏ Pear

Hair Analysis

HAIR DESCRIPTION

Which best describes the texture of your hair?

☐ Each individual hair is strong and thick.

☐ It often appears bushy or wiry.

☐ My hair is not fine or coarse.

☐ Each strand appears average in thickness.

☐ Each hair is fine.

☐ Each hair is fine and breaks easily.

Which best describes the degree of curl in your hair?

☐ Very curly

☐ Curly

☐ Wavy

☐ Slightly wavy

☐ Straight

Which best describes the thickness of your hair?

☐ Thick

☐ Medium

☐ Thin

Which best describes your hair and scalp condition?

☐ Dry

☐ Normal

☐ Oily

Which best describes the condition of your hair?

☐ Shiny and healthy.

☐ Highlights or color.

☐ Permed or straightened.

☐ Bleached and colored.

☐ Permed and colored.

☐ Straightened and colored.

☐ Damaged by treatment or environment.

Skin Analysis

YOUR SKIN

Select the ones that best describe your skin

How would you describe your facial pores?
- ❏ Very small, not noticeable
- ❏ Fine to average
- ❏ Small to average
- ❏ Medium to large at T zone only
- ❏ Medium to large
- ❏ Large

How often do you experience dry or peeling skin (when not using moisturizers)?
- ❏ Often
- ❏ Occasionally
- ❏ Rarely
- ❏ Occasionally in some areas
- ❏ Rarely to never
- ❏ Never

Does your skin feel dry and tight (when not treated)?
- ❏ Often
- ❏ Occasionally
- ❏ Occasionally in some areas
- ❏ Rarely
- ❏ Rarely to never
- ❏ Never

How often do you experience breakouts?
- ❏ Very rarely
- ❏ Rarely
- ❏ Frequently
- ❏ Occasionally
- ❏ Sometimes
- ❏ Constantly

What is your age?
- ❏ 65 or older
- ❏ 45–54
- ❏ 20–29
- ❏ 55–64
- ❏ 30–44
- ❏ 20 or younger

How would you describe your facial lines?
- ❏ Many
- ❏ Some to many
- ❏ Some
- ❏ Few to none
- ❏ None

How would you describe your skin elasticity and tone?
- ❏ Poor
- ❏ Average to poor
- ❏ Average
- ❏ Average to good
- ❏ Very good
- ❏ Excellent

Does your skin look and feel oily shortly after cleansing?
- ❏ Rarely or never
- ❏ Sometimes in T zone
- ❏ Rarely if ever
- ❏ Often in T zone
- ❏ Most of the time
- ❏ Often

How would you describe the appearance of your skin?
- ❏ Smooth, dry, often flaky, parched, or chapped
- ❏ Sensitive, thin, ruddy (may have broken capillaries, rough in spots)
- ❏ Smooth, supple, mattelike, clear
- ❏ Shiny on T zone and normal to dry in other areas
- ❏ Coarse, shiny, oily or moist, thick
- ❏ Clogged pores, pimples or blackheads, bumps under skin, oily

Index

African-American color types
  bright, 47
  cool, 50
  deep, 45
  light, 46
  muted, 48
  warm, 49
AHAs
  See alpha hydroxy acids (AHAs);
  glycolic acid peels
alpha hydroxy acids (AHAs), 70, 75
  See also glycolic acid peels
angular face shapes, 15
  accentuating positives of, 16
  best hairstyles for, 20–21
  angular hairline treatments, 21
antioxidants in skin-care products, 75–76
Asian color types
  bright, 47
  cool, 50
  deep, 45
  light, 46
  muted, 48
  warm, 49

bad hair days, 19
beta glucan, 68
BHA (salicylic acid), 70, 75
blush
  applying, 86
  choosing, 97
Botox, 73
bright color types, 44, 47
  best makeup colors for, 84, 90
  complementary hair colors for, 58
brightness, 43

Caucasian color types
  bright, 44, 47
  cool, 44, 50
  deep, 44, 45
  light, 44, 46

muted, 44, 48
warm, 44, 49
"challenges"
  hairstyle solutions for, 19–25
clarity, 43
cleansers, 74–75
color analysis, 41–51
color blocking (hair), 60
color characteristics, 42–43
  dominant, 44–51
  makeup for different, 84–85, 88–93
  See also color types
color shaping (hair), 59–60
color types, 42–43
  bright, 44, 47
    complementary hair colors for, 58
  cool, 44, 50
    complementary hair colors for, 59
  deep, 44, 45
    complementary hair colors for, 57
  light, 44, 46
    complementary hair colors for, 57
  muted, 44, 48
    complementary hair colors for, 58
  warm, 44, 49
    complementary hair colors for, 58
  See also color characteristics
coloring
  See hair coloring
concealer
  applying, 86
  choosing, 95–96
conditioners, new, 30
conditioning
  color-treated hair, 62
  hair, 29–30
cool color types, 44, 50
  best makeup colors for, 85, 93
  complementary hair colors for, 59
cosmetic surgery, 71

curling eyelashes, 99
curved face shapes, 15
  accentuating positives of, 16
  best hairstyles for, 22–23
  curved hairline treatments, 23

deep color types, 44, 45
  complementary hair colors for, 57
  best makeup colors for, 84, 88
depth, 43
dermatologists, 71–72
diamond face shape
  best hairstyles for, 20
  defining, 15
Donsuki Salon, 11, 16, 27, 53, 74
double identity (hair coloring), 60
dry skin, 70
Duggan, Suki, 11, 16–17, 27–30, 37, 53, 60

electro-stimulation, 74
enzyme peels, 80
exfoliants, 75
eye cream, 79–80
eyebrow pencil
  applying, 87
eyebrows
  balancing with hair color, 61, 96
  tweezing, 97–98
eyelashes
  curling, 99
eyeliner
  applying, 87
  choosing, 98
eyes
  makeup application charts, 100–102
eyeshadow
  applying, 87
  choosing, 98, 99

face shapes, 14
  accentuating positives of, 16
  angular, 15

balancing with hairstyles, 17–18
  "challenges" and hairstyle solutions, 19–25
  curved, 15
  defining, 16–17
foundation
  applying, 86
  choosing, 94–95

glazing (hair), 61
glossing (hair), 61
glycolic acid peels, 71–72
grape seed extract, 68

hair, 27–39
  caring for colored, 61–62
  cleansing, 29
  conditioning and moisturizing, 29–30
  conditioning products for, 30
  facts, 28
  styling products, 29, 30–31
hair color, 51
  balancing eyebrows with, 61, 96
  complementary, 51, 55–59
hair coloring, 53–65
  for blondes, 63
  for brunettes, 65
  caring for, 61–62
  fashion show, 63–65
  fashions, 54, 55
  for redheads, 64
  salon versus at-home, 62
  techniques, 59–61
  terminology, 60
hair painting, 60
hair types, 31–39
  coarse and curly, 32, 37
  coarse, straight, and thick, 33, 37
  fine and wavy, 36, 38
  fine, straight, and thick, 35, 38
  fine, straight, and thin, 34, 37–38

hairlines
  angular, 21
  curved, 23
hairstyles
  angular, 18
    for angular face shapes, 20–21
  angular hairline treatments, 21
  asymmetrical cut, 21
  balancing face shape with, 17–18
  blunt cut, 21
  bobbed, 21
  for coarse and curly hair, 32, 37
  for coarse, straight, and thick hair, 33, 37
  complementary, 13–25
  curved, 18
  for curved face shapes, 22–23
  curved hairline treatments, 23
  for fine and wavy hair, 36, 38
  for fine, straight, and thick hair, 35, 38
  for fine, straight, and thin hair, 34, 37–38
  off face style, 21
  short feathered cuts, 23
  soft waves and curls with blunt cut, 23
  softened curls, 23
  solutions for face-shape "challenges," 19–25
  straight with tapered ends, 23
heart face shape
  best hairstyles for, 22
  defining, 15
highlighting (hair), 59

injections, 73

lash curling, 99
light color types, 44, 46
  best makeup colors for, 84, 89
  complementary hair colors for, 57

lip pencil
  applying, 87
  choosing, 99, 105
  See also lips
lips
  makeup application charts, 103–4
  See also lip pencil; lipstick
lipstick
  applying, 87
  choosing, 99, 105
  See also lips

makeup, 83–106
  applying, 86–93
  blush, 86, 97
  choosing correct products, 94–98, 102–5
  color types and, 84–85, 88–93
  concealer, 86, 95–96
  for different occasions, 106
  evening, 105, 106
  eyeshadow, 87, 98
  foundation, 86, 94–95
  lipstick and lip pencil, 87, 99, 105
  mascara, 87, 99
  powder, 86, 96–97
  top five products used by age, 85
makeup application charts
  eyes, 100–102
  lips, 103–4
mascara
  applying, 87
  choosing, 99
masks, 80
microdermabrasion, 72
moisturizers (skin), 78–79
moisturizing hair, 29–30
muted color types, 44, 48
  best makeup colors for, 84, 91
  complementary hair colors for, 58

oval face shape
  best hairstyles for, 22
  defining, 15

panthenol, 68
pear face shape
  best hairstyles for, 22
  defining, 15
peels
  enzyme, 80
  glycolic acid, 71–72
  other, 72–73
plastic surgery, 71
powder
  applying, 86
  choosing, 96–97

rectangle face shape
  best hairstyles for, 20
  defining, 15
Renova, 75–76
Retin A, 75–76
retinol, 76
round face shape
  best hairstyles for, 22
  defining, 15

salicylic acid (BHA), 70, 75
scrubs, 80
self-tanners, 80–81
shampoo, 29
skin
  dry, 70
  healthy, 69–70
  See also color types; skin care
skin care, 67–81
  professional, 70–73
skin color
  See color types, 42–43
skin-care products
  antioxidants in, 75–76
  cleansers, 74–75
  enzyme peels, 80
  exfoliants, 75
  eye cream, 79–80
  ingredients found in, 68
  masks and scrubs, 80
  moisturizers, 78–79
  self-tanners, 80–81
  sunscreens, 79
  toners, 75

top five products used by age, 85
  vitamin C in, 76–78
skin-care routine
  basic, 73–81
  checklist, 78
smudging (hair), 60
square face shape
  best hairstyles for, 20
  defining, 15
styling products
  new, 29
  using, 30–31
sun damage, 70
sunscreens, 70, 79
superoxide dismutase, 68

teeth
  veneers and bonding for, 77
  whitening, 77
toners, 75
triangle face shape
  best hairstyles for, 20
  defining, 15

undertones, 42–43

vitamins in skin-care products, 68, 75–78
vitamin A, 68, 75–76
vitamin C, 68, 76–78
vitamin E, 68

warm color types, 44, 49
  best makeup colors for, 85, 92
  complementary hair colors for, 58
well-dressed
  defining, 13–14
wrinkles, 70
  treating with Botox, 73
  treating with electro-stimulation, 74
  treating with glycolic acid peels and other peels, 72–74
  treating with injections, 73
  treating with microdermabrasion, 72